PRAISE FOR

Who's In Your Social Network?

Brilliant commentary on what we are all struggling with in a way that feeds the Facebook monster in all of us . . .and leaves us convicted about that same beast! Pam is a prophet who holds nothing back. No legalism here, but she does force social mediums to bend to the truth of God!

Dannah Gresh
Bestselling author and founder of purefreedom.org

It's no surprise that Pam Stenzel has hit a homerun with *Who's In Your Social Network?*—she's the most sought-after female speaker on sexuality, purity and sexual consequences to today's generation! Pam is the expert. She knows that 38 percent of teens today are sending or receiving sexually suggestive messages and that most of them have no idea that their social media habits are grossly affecting their character, reputation and their future. If you're wondering how what you're sexting at age 14 can affect your chances of getting into the college of your dreams at 19—or how what you're posting on Facebook right now can affect your first job interview for the career of your choice at age 23—*this is a must read!*

Susie Shellenberger
Editor of *SUSIE Magazine*, author and speaker

Pam and Melissa understand the often-addictive qualities of today's media climate as well as our obsessive desire to share and be validated online. "I post, therefore I am" seems to be the cogito of our age. This powerful, important book looks directly into the soul of entertainment vying for the attention of a generation used to scrolling through Facebook updates. I've never read anything like it.

Bob Smithouser
Senior editor with PluggedIn.com

When we're young, we think we are invincible and that nothing we do will have long-term repercussions. Experience teaches us just the opposite, but how do we get today's texting, tweeting, tech-savvy youth to realize that what they say and do online could follow them forever? *Who's in Your Social Network?* answers that question and also hits teens, parents and educators right between the eyes with the truth about the impact of social media.

Teresa Tomeo

Syndicated Catholic talk show host, bestselling Catholic author, and motivational speaker

Who's In Your Social Network?

Pam Stenzel
& Melissa Nesdahl
Authors of *Nobody Told Me!*

Who's In Your Social Network?

**Understand the Risks Associated with
Modern Media and Social Networking
and How It Can Impact Your Character
and Relationships**

Regal

**From Gospel Light
Ventura, California, U.S.A.**

Published by Regal
From Gospel Light
Ventura, California, U.S.A.
www.regalbooks.com
Printed in the U.S.A.

Stenzel, Pam, 1965-
Who's in your social network? : understanding the risks associated with media and
social networking and how it can impact your character and relationships / Pam Stenzel,
Melissa Nesdahl.
    p. cm.
Includes bibliographical references (p.   ) and index.
ISBN 978-0-8307-6054-1 (trade paper : alk. paper)
1. Christianity and culture. 2. Mass media—Influence. 3. Social networks—Influence.
I. Nesdahl, Melissa. II. Title.
BR115.C8S733 2011
261.5'2—dc23
2011028470

Rights for publishing this book outside the U.S.A. or in non-English languages are
administered by Gospel Light Worldwide, an international not-for-profit ministry.
For additional information, please visit www.glww.org, email info@glww.org, or write
to Gospel Light Worldwide, 1957 Eastman Avenue, Ventura, CA 93003, U.S.A.

To order copies of this book and other Regal products in bulk quantities,
please contact us at 1-800-446-7735.

Dedication

This book is dedicated to all who were brave enough to share their struggles, honest enough to ask their questions, and bold enough to use today's technology to glorify the Lord.

Pam Stenzel and Melissa Nesdahl

1 mutual follower
Interested In: Clothes,
Fashion, Modeling
+ Follow Me

200 mutual followers
Interested In: Boys,
Friends, Family
+ Follow Me

1 mutual follower
Interested In: Nothing
+ Follow Me

5 mutual followers
Interested In: Friends,
Christian Clubs
+ Follow Me

5 mutual followers
Interested In: Boys,
A good time, Fun!
+ Follow Me

7 mutual followers
Interested In: Revenge,
Payback, Who Cares!
+ Follow Me

67 mutual followers
Interested In: Boys,
Science, Money
+ Follow Me

Contents

3 mutual followers
Interested In: Family,
Going to college
+ Follow Me

2 mutual followers
Interested In: Getting
out of high school
+ Follow Me

29 mutual followers
Interested In: Grades,
Sports, Boys, College
+ Follow Me

81 mutual followers
Interested In: Boys,
Sexting, Gossip
+ Follow Me

10 mutual followers
Interested In: Girls,
Teasing, Mocking
+ Follow Me

105 mutual followers
Interested In: Clubs,
Disappearing, Cutting
+ Follow Me

105 mutual followers
Interested In: Boys,
Experimenting, Fun!
+ Follow Me

Once school is out, I am pretty much a media maniac. I know it affects my sleep, because there is always something more to look at, another person to chat with, or one more game to play.

Do you actually think that what I am doing now affects my life-long character? Give me a break! I'm only 14. Tweens should be able to be tweens. We can "grow up" later.

Introduction

From the time you get up in the morning to the minute you fall asleep at night, you are bombarded with media. Your iPod alarm wakes you up, feeding your brain its first message of the day. Then you sit down at the breakfast table and pick up the remote. What do you choose to watch? On your way out the door, you grab your cell phone and text your friends. Whether you drive or take the bus, music is playing through the car stereo or your ear buds.

Although it seems like our minds should be on overload by this point, they are not. We are immersed in a society driven by technology. We use it for education, connection and fun. We need it to engage in this world. So, you go into the classroom and use computers, and then you follow that up with study time (often including online research) and Facebook or other social networking sites when you get home. Is what you are viewing positive and pure? Is what you are posting kind and uplifting?

As the day draws to a close, you actually are tired, so you seek out mindless entertainment. Some will choose to put in a DVD or watch TV, so they can simply enjoy being entertained. Others will turn on their gaming systems and network online with others to provide a virtual gaming party minus the popcorn. Either way, while your guard is down, your mind is absorbing the messages of all that you see and play. Are they positive and inspiring, or are they violent and harmful?

Media can be a wonderful means to glorify God and connect with others, but it can also be horribly destructive. Since it IS going to be part of your life, you must CHOOSE how you will use it. In Romans 12:2 we are encouraged, "Don't become so well-adjusted to your culture that you fit into it without even thinking. Instead, fix your attention on God. You'll be changed from the inside out. Readily recognize what he wants from you, and quickly respond to it. Unlike the culture around you, always dragging you down to its level of immaturity, God brings the best out of you, develops well-formed maturity in you" (*THE MESSAGE*). The challenge is to be in this world but not of it, so that you will be MATURE!

For many years, we have heard teens say, "I had no idea this would be the result of my media choices. Now I'm so deep in sin it feels too late." But we've also seen many teenagers using social networking and media for good. Our hope is that this book will bring healing to your past and help raise awareness for the future. You will no longer see the media as something to fear or question, but rather will feel empowered to make healthy choices and use media for your benefit and HIS glory, bringing life and joy to yourself and everyone around you. This is your opportunity to heed the warnings and encouragement of your peers, as well as our teaching, to use the gift of media to change the world. Never before has there been so much opportunity to impact the world from the privacy of your own home.

Will the media you consume take you down, or will you take down the strongholds of the enemy by fighting this battle and winning? We pray you will be equipped with all you need to fight this good fight!

Pam Stenzel and Melissa Nesdahl

Chapter 1

Asess Your Media Health: Is a Diet Necessary?

 Pam: Whatever has our attention WILL influence us. You cannot live "above the influence."
Comment On This · Love This · Share with Friends

 Tony: I love those commercials. They are telling us to rise above influences around us.
Comment On This · Love This · Share with Friends

 Pam: Hey, Tony. Stop and think about it for a second. Aren't they USING media messages to "influence" me to be "above the influence"? Just sayin'!
Comment On This · Love This · Share with Friends

 Lexa: I heard you speak at my school last year. When you were there you said, "What you are looking at on your computer, what you are sending on your phone, and all the other choices you make today—that is the trust that you are handing your future spouse someday." I went home and took an honest look at my life. Quite frankly, until that moment, I didn't think much about the TV shows I watched or care about the lyrics to my music. I just went with the "popular" thing. My Facebook page had pictures of me in a bikini my parents would kill me for posting. Pam, I am a Christian, but somehow I separated faith from media culture. I thought I was just using media to fit in, connect and "belong."

But, after hearing you speak, I realized it represented the core of who I was . . . and I needed to change. I ditched a few of my shows and started listening to a different music station. It's funny how changing the lyrics running through your head from worldly stuff to Christian messages impacts your perspective during the day. I also started thinking about my future spouse before posting pictures on my Facebook page. Since then, I feel better about myself. I had no idea I was being dragged down by it all, but I'm thankful that you removed the blinders.

I'm closer to Christ than I have ever been, and I feel confident that the trust I will hand my husband someday is far more trustworthy today than it was a year ago. That was only a small part of your talk, but it changed my life. Thank you for addressing the topic!

Comment On This · Love This · Share with Friends

Pam: Thanks for sharing your story! You are in good company. None of us is above the influence. We are all being "influenced" daily, hourly, even minute by minute. The source of that influence can change. The amount of time with our influences can change. But, one fact remains: We are all receiving thousands of messages a day that impact our thoughts, values, beliefs and behaviors. Good for you for honestly assessing your influences so that you can change the negative to positive and be a person of character, living out a more godly life!

Comment On This · Love This · Share with Friends

✍ Note: Exercise in a Bottle. Advertising researchers have determined a time at night (around 2 A.M.) when over-tired brains are more likely to believe anything you pitch them. Although I'm embarrassed to publicly admit it, I have fallen prey to their brilliant scheme. One sleepless night in a hotel, I actually picked up the phone and purchased a product called "Exercise in a Bottle." According to the infomercial, I would no longer need to exercise, which I loathe more than a root canal, because if I simply took this little pill, it would be "just as if" I had actually exercised.

As you can imagine, I was ecstatic to receive my bottle of pills and watch the weight just melt off. My life would be forever changed for just $19.95! *Wrong.* They lied! How had I so easily believed them? How did I fall prey to such a ridiculous claim?

First of all, the appeal caused me to watch and partake without thinking about it. I didn't ask myself if the claims made were rational or not. I just wanted a quick, easy solution. Oftentimes with social media we do the same thing. Prior to turning on a television show, sending a text, playing a game or pulling up a website, we don't ask ourselves if the messages they are sending are healthy—we just do it.

Weight loss, like so many other things in life, is *earned*. It takes effort. Just like I needed to change my attitude about exercise—it was time to stop cutting corners and whining about it—we often need an attitude adjustment concerning the opportunities we have to build our character and strengthen our walk with Christ.

There will be many media temptations each day, but James 1:2-4 says, "Consider it pure joy, my brothers and sisters, whenever you face trials of many kinds, because you know that the testing of your faith produces perseverance. Let perseverance finish its work so that you may be mature and complete, not lacking anything." Through trials we have the opportunity to make right choices and strengthen our faith. We can take the (sometimes difficult) steps to build maturity. As we do these things, we achieve integrity and can fully live out the life God intends for us.

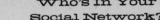
Oftentimes we want "character in a bottle," but great character qualities like honesty, respect, courage, wisdom and humility will never be just handed to us. They are developed over time and with effort. If we truly want to become champions of the faith, we must "count it all joy" that we are being MADE more like Christ with every trial and test. We must give thanks for the hard work demanded of us. As we confront media, we must make conscientious, thoughtful choices, trusting in His promise that He who began this good work in me will be faithful to complete it (see Philippians 1:6)!

Abby: How awesome! I've never thought about the testing of my character as a gift. Whenever I open up magazines and see the scantily clad fashion models, I only think of being stylish.

Comment On This · Love This · Share with Friends

Pam: This is one example of the rubber meeting the road. Will you take fashion advice from a magazine that lacks moral integrity, or will you stand strong against the tasteless ways of the world? Your body is a temple of the Holy Spirit (see 1 Corinthians 6:19). Are your choices honoring Him? This is a cool moment! You get to *decide* if you will opt for cheap worldly satisfaction that results in diminished self-respect. Or, you can turn your eyes away, invest time in finding some trendy but modest clothes, and feel good about both the way you look AND the way you are pleasing God.

Comment On This · Love This · Share with Friends

Joe: Cool comparison, Pam! Thank you for challenging us!

Comment On This · Love This · Share with Friends

Meghan: I read your note, and I agree with your talk that sex is an intimate moment that only a husband and wife should share. When I was 12, I promised God that I would wait for my husband. My problem is, I tend to read books and articles about sex. I don't lust over anyone. I just imagine myself pleasing someone that's going to be my husband. Is that wrong? Even though I know I shouldn't read those stories and stuff, I like them! And I feel horrible because of it. I don't understand why, no matter how hard I try to stop, I continue to read them. It upsets me because I don't want God to look down upon me and frown. Is there anything I can do?

Comment On This · Love This · Share with Friends

Pam: I appreciate your honesty. When I was young, my grandfather shared this poem with me:

Vice is a monster of so fearful a mien,
As to be hated, upon merely being seen;
But seen too oft, familiar with its faces;
One first endures, then fondles, then embraces.
(Alexander Pope)

I can tell from your words that you know reading these materials is wrong, but you started looking at them, grew attached and are now struggling to separate from this vice.

Your guilt comes from loving God but failing to make decisions He would want for your life. Contrary to popular belief, our most powerful sex organ isn't used for procreation. It's our mind—and you are imagining yourself with someone to whom you aren't married. To feel better about (and strengthen) your character, you need to rid yourself of these reading materials. You know reading these things is chipping away at your character. Throw them away today and refuse to pick them up again! By focusing your mind on what is right and pure, you will better respect the spouse God has for you, and the intimacy will be far greater than you could have ever imagined!

Comment On This · Love This · Share with Friends

 Pam: "Watch your thoughts; they become words. Watch your words; they become actions. Watch your actions; they become habits. Watch your habits; they become character. Watch your character; it becomes your destiny" (Author Unknown).

Comment On This · Love This · Share with Friends

 Gina: This was what I needed to see today! We are watching your "sex talk" at school. There is this guy, Cade, who is in the eighth grade just like me. He's had sex with like six girls, and he's been asking me non-stop if I would ever sleep with him. I know that's bad, but yes, I have had thoughts about it. I think at this point I am just curious to see what it is like. I am afraid my curiosity will get the best of me. I haven't answered him, but I flirt a lot. I suppose I should stop.

Comment On This · Love This · Share with Friends

 Pam: Gina, if your mind is entertaining these thoughts and you haven't answered him, you are on a one-way track to trouble. You NEED to tell this guy no and stay far away from him. Clearly he's trying to use you. Your personal integrity is on the line. Stop this freight train before it leads to disaster!

Comment On This · Love This · Share with Friends

Catherine: Don't feel bad, Gina! I'm waiting for "Mr. Right" and I haven't even kissed a guy, but I've had guys ask me to hang and "hook up." I can relate to your curiosity. I see stuff in movies, and sometimes I think I want that.

Comment On This • Love This • Share with Friends

Joe: You girls ever heard the phrase "curiosity killed the cat"? I'm waiting for my wife, and if you give in to this "curiosity" now, the guys you want might not want you later. It's not rocket science.

Comment On This • Love This • Share with Friends

💚 Maria's Story

 There is this one boy in my class I love a lot. We have cybersex often because we both like using words to excite each other and make one another happy. We both agreed to go out on a date. Now I'm a little nervous. Just the other day, we were on our bus ride back from a class field trip. At dinner, he started touching my leg. I really liked it, so I did the same to his. It seemed like innocent fun. Then, when we got on the bus, we went towards the back, and he started acting out more of our IM (instant messenger) conversations. He said he would never do anything to make me uncomfortable, and I didn't feel like anything was wrong at the time, but when I got home I looked in the mirror and didn't recognize myself. How had typed words led to my allowing things I didn't think I'd do? I guess the seemingly harmless IMs were actually harmful because they managed to change me into a person that I didn't want to be.

📰 **Newsflash:** "39% of all teens . . . are sending or posting sexually suggestive messages." Additionally, 38% recognize that "exchanging sexually suggestive content makes dating or hooking up with others more likely."[1]

 AJ: I would like to know how you address the issue of desire with teenagers. I feel like it's the biggest problem we face. Sometimes I become so consumed by an idea that I find myself ignoring things I know are true.

Comment On This • Love This • Share with Friends

 Pam: First of all, the DESIRE is not bad, but when you attach your DESIRE to something GOD has not provided to meet the need, then you have big problems. For example, your desire to "love and be loved" is given by God, but when you fill that need and desire with empty sex and images of sex, this becomes SIN. God has provided for your every need. You need to trust HIM with your desire rather than try to fill those desires your own way. The problem with misplaced desire actually stems from a lack of self-control and the issue of indefinite boundaries. If a person has made a decision to stay away from something known to be dangerous—and sticks to that decision—the desire does NOT become an issue. It is only when we are wishy-washy and let our minds wander that we get into trouble.

Meditating on Scripture is a powerful method of combating unhealthy desire. When your foundation is built on Christ's Word, you can withstand all worldly trials. Psalm 1:1-3 says, "How blessed is the man who does not walk in the counsel of the wicked, nor stand in the path of sinners, nor sit in the seat of scoffers! But his delight is in the law of the LORD, and in His law he meditates day and night. He will be like a tree firmly planted by streams of water, which yields its fruit in its season and its leaf does not wither; and in whatever he does, he prospers" (*NASB*). Studying the Bible will help you know the Lord's desires for your life and hold on to what is good while rejecting every kind of evil (see 1 Thessalonians 5:21-22).

Comment On This · Love This · Share with Friends

 Pam: "Character is the result of two things: mental attitude and the way we spend our time" (Elbert Hubbard). So I ask you: How much time are you spending bonding with media each week?

Comment On This · Love This · Share with Friends

 Alana: I don't have any limits on media. I'm old enough to monitor myself. My parents think it's ridiculous, but they're totally old school. Just a little TV for them!

Comment On This · Love This · Share with Friends

 Chase: I spend most of my day with some form of electronics. I text and talk on my phone, watch TV, play PlayStation and check my Facebook daily. In fact, if my computer, phone or TV broke, I'm pretty sure I'd go nuts.

Comment On This · Love This · Share with Friends

 Devin: Once school is out, I am pretty much a media maniac. I've got my computer and TV in my room, so I can play Xbox LIVE, log onto Myspace and everything else. Honestly, I know it affects my sleep, because there is always something more to look at, another person to chat with, or one more game to play.

Comment On This · Love This · Share with Friends

Ashley: Chase, you'd "go nuts" without these things? How sad. There is so much more to life, my friend!

Comment On This · Love This · Share with Friends

 Pam: Check it out! I just read that the average student today consumes 7.5 hours of media per day. When multitasking was included, the number jumped to 10 hours and 45 minutes![2]

Comment On This · Love This · Share with Friends

📝 **Note: Total Media Use.** Among all 8- to 18-year-olds, average amount of time spent with each medium in a typical day (hours/minutes):

Average Number of Hours Teens Spend per Day

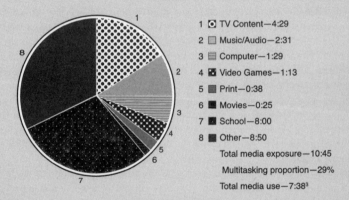

1. 🔘 TV Content—4:29
2. ⬜ Music/Audio—2:31
3. 📄 Computer—1:29
4. 🎮 Video Games—1:13
5. ⬛ Print—0:38
6. ⬛ Movies—0:25
7. ⬛ School—8:00
8. ⬛ Other—8:50

Total media exposure—10:45

Multitasking proportion—29%

Total media use—7:38[3]

Over seven hours a day, seven days a week, adds up to more than a full-time job! I charted out the data, and when you factor in an eight-hour school day, you barely have more than eight hours for "other," such as sleeping, eating, and participating in sports or other extra-curricular activities.

 Todd: Wow! Seeing time averages in this form is mind-blowing.

Comment On This · Love This · Share with Friends

 Sara: How sad that "other" would have to include homework, sports, time outdoors and even sleeping, and it's hardly any more than the amount of time spent with media. Yikes!

Comment On This · Love This · Share with Friends

Tonya: This might explain why my parents aren't happy with my grades. ☺

Comment On This · Love This · Share with Friends

 Pam: I hoped that seeing this pie chart would make you think. Your time is precious. Are you treating it that way?

Comment On This · Love This · Share with Friends

📰 **Newsflash:** No more than two hours of quality entertainment (screen time) per day is recommended.[4]

📓 **Note: What's Your Intake?** In order for the discussion in the rest of the chapters to make a difference in our real lives, we have to be able to be honest with ourselves about what media we are taking in every day.

I'm reminded of ways I handle other important responsibilities in life. We are a very health-conscious society. Whenever I go to the doctor, there is a brightly colored food plate poster on the wall telling me healthy quantities of each type of food to eat. As I enter the grocery store, I immediately note labeled health food sections. Restaurants now include cute little symbols on their menus to let me know which items qualify as heart-friendly or low-calorie.

You can probably guess from my "Exercise in a Bottle" experience that weight and food intake are prevalent on my mind. Truthfully, I utterly detest dealing with diet issues, but I knew I needed to do something (besides taking a pill that didn't work), so I decided that I would check out Weight Watchers. After all, Jennifer Hudson looks amazing!

Once I paid my online joining fee, I downloaded the really cool app for my iPhone that helps me track my points. The app is cool—what's not so cool (or at least, not so fun) is that I am required to enter EVERY LITTLE THING I put in my mouth. No mercy. Even a stick of gum must be counted.

Weight Watchers operates on a point system. Each food or drink item has a point value, and I am allowed so many points in a day. If I go over my point allotment one day, I need to consume less the next day.

When I first started, I thought I could get away with estimating. I rationalized that my points would at least be within the ballpark and I'd see results. But I wasn't reaching my goals and soon became frustrated with the lack of progress. Then I realized that my "estimating" was sabotaging my diet. I was estimating way too low! Unless I decided to be REALLY honest about my eating habits, I was never going to lose the weight and reach the goals I had set for myself.

I think we do the same thing with our media intake. We know that what we put IN our minds is going to affect WHO WE ARE and will be reflected in our character, but we don't want to be honest with ourselves about HOW MUCH WE ARE PUTTING IN!

Angie: I think I get home from school and turn on the TV without thinking. If I were to keep track of how much I watch, I might be embarrassed!
Comment On This · Love This · Share with Friends

 Pam: Angie, relax! I'm sure you aren't the only person who feels this way. Many of us are cramming into our brains the equivalent of a steady diet of Twinkies, Mountain Dew and Double Whoppers with extra cheese, and then we wonder how we became 500 pounds of pure nastiness. Our character is on the line!
Comment On This · Love This · Share with Friends

 Pam: How would you rate your media consumption? Is what you are digesting healthy?
Comment On This · Love This · Share with Friends

 Travis: Are you anti-media? I mean, saying that what we are looking at, sending and listening to impacts our character seems a little overboard.
Comment On This · Love This · Share with Friends

 Pam: Let me very clear. I am not telling you that all media is bad. Just like eating isn't bad (it is in fact necessary to live), taking in media is not bad in and of itself. However, we have to look carefully at HOW MUCH we are taking in and the nutritional value of what we are choosing to consume! Basically, we need to remove "junk food" and fattening calories from our diets while keeping those things that nourish us. The key is balance.

There are many benefits to media today. Texting allows for quick, non-invasive conversations. Smartphones will help you get from point *A* to point *B* without misdirection. On weekends, families gather around the Wii and share in lively bowling tournaments. Google has allowed people to get on the computer and, with the simplicity of a key word or phrase, access a wealth of data well beyond an encyclopedia article. Truthful information can help you better understand the real risks of premarital sex, drugs and alcohol, and the list goes on.

On the other hand, Ecclesiastes 7:4 warns, "The heart of fools is in the house of pleasure." When these media are used to dehumanize or harm another human being, we are impacted, whether we recognize it or not. If we focus on music and television that send messages that our bodies don't deserve respect, we slowly begin to believe what we hear. If we play games that promote violence, we harden our hearts to the real pain that defines some people's existence. If we bully others on social networking sites, we become disconnected from humanity. If we look at pornography or sext pictures and messages, we reduce people made in the image of God to a collection of body parts. We NEED empathy so that we don't become people who forget the feelings and value of others. Our actions ALWAYS affect the other, and a person of character says, "I know that what I'm doing impacts you, and that matters."

The key is prayerfully considering what you are looking at and seriously asking yourself if your time with it is affecting real-life relationships, one-on-one conversations, academic success and/or mental wellbeing. You MUST exercise wisdom.

Trust me, Travis, I LOVE my media. I text friends and family and update my Facebook fan page, but I use it for good—a ministry—and that is the difference!

Comment On This · Love This · Share with Friends

Note: Pearls in the Media Muck. I was paging through *Charisma* magazine and loved this challenge to all of us. Read the excerpt and think!

I used to get paid to watch movies. And sit in front of a TV. And listen to music. And play video games. In fact, if I were still at my previous workplace, my job would now include hanging out on Facebook, Twitter, YouTube and the like. Yep, I once earned a paycheck by consuming media all week long. . . .

Fortunately, I don't remember most of the filth I took in for others' sake. But that isn't the case for the average teen, child or adult who's now only a click away from having unlimited perversion in any form, delivered on any medium, embedded in their brains. Technology has always ushered in a wave of immorality, yet today we find a unique problem: a generation clueless as to why such depravity is even wrong in the first place.

Something's seriously amiss when male students at a Bible college see nothing wrong with taking photos of their genitalia during class and texting them to female friends. That's a true story, and sadly not unlike others I've heard involving young Christians, many of whom have become walking reflections of whatever content is on their iPod, iPhone or iPad.

This isn't just a youth issue. As media consumption becomes ubiquitous for every age group, our appetite for entertainment grows more insatiable—and our morals continue to decline. We can blame Hollywood all we want, but it's no longer the core generator of content—we are. (Thank you, social media.)

I'm not pulling out the overused "evil media" card, nor am I advocating for believers to tune out pop culture. I am, however, begging us to develop the ability to discern right from wrong amid our being oversaturated with content. Remember, media—social or not—aren't the problem; they're just vehicles. It's the content *in* those media that's often not only problematic, it's mimicked to the extent of becoming the new cultural norm.

As "vehicles" for the Holy Spirit, we can present a different standard and culture: the kingdom of God. Jesus likened this kingdom to finding a pearl in a field of dirt. We know the fields of today's media world can be mucky. But rather than mindlessly wandering through the sludge, let's develop enough discernment to find the pearls.[5]

Nicole: Reading this made me think of *Glee.* That show promotes teen promiscuity and homosexuality as though they were normal. These messages are pounded in our brains over and over weekly in the name of a musical. I finally realized this and quit watching.
Comment On This · Love This · Share with Friends

Tia: In Philippians 4:8, Paul says, "Finally, brothers and sisters, whatever is true, whatever is noble, whatever is right, whatever is pure, whatever is lovely, whatever is admirable—if anything is excellent or praiseworthy—think about such things."
Comment On This · Love This · Share with Friends

Pam: Thanks for sharing this Scripture. It is perfect for each of us to use as a barometer when using social media!
Comment On This · Love This · Share with Friends

Anna: It's not like we don't see and hear worse at school. Not watching the show isn't guarding us from much.
Comment On This · Love This · Share with Friends

Jed: Anna, you're missing the point. The arts are the most powerful culture-changing tool known to man. It's not that it's not okay in TV but it is okay in real life. It's that if you want to shift a culture, you portray how you want it to be in media and music, because that's what trends follow. Most TV shows these days have sex outside of marriage in them, and that normalizes it and makes it an everyday thing to kids and teens. When you watch a movie or TV show, your guards are naturally down, and you accept things more easily than you normally would, because you lose the sense

of realness to it. We as children of THE Creator should be the most creative force on the planet instead of trying to copy what the world likes. Business holds power, but the arts shape cultures.
Comment On This · Love This · Share with Friends

Pam: Wow! AWESOME, Jed!
Comment On This · Love This · Share with Friends

Pam: If we aren't willing to take an HONEST look at our media habits, we will not be able to win the battle for the mind. We have to be ruthless in our assessment and committed to doing the work it will take to keep our minds pure—which will fortify good character and enable us to live lives of holiness.
Comment On This · Love This · Share with Friends

Danya: Do you actually think that what I am doing now affects my life-long character? Give me a break! I'm only 14. Teens should be able to be teens. We can "grow up" later.
Comment On This · Love This · Share with Friends

Josh: As someone who has made some bad choices, I know that Pam is right. I used to look up pornography on my computer in my room. My parents had no idea. There was something inside of me telling me it was wrong when I was doing it, but I continued to choose to look at it.

One day my parents' computer crashed, and my mom went to use my computer. Out of curiosity, she checked my site viewing. Not only was I busted, but I was also in major trouble. At first I blew up about how she had violated my privacy and told her she had no right to look at what she did. But my anger didn't matter to her. She cried and told me she was "worried about my heart." I thought she meant because I was livid mad at her.

My parents immediately removed the computer from my room and put it in the living room. Filters were installed to limit what I could view, and my parents made me meet with my pastor and confess it to him. I felt like a moron, but they'd already told him the truth so I couldn't lie my way out of it. My parents checked my browsing history daily, and I had to meet with my pastor weekly.

Within a short time, I came to better understand why my mom was worried about my "heart." When I wasn't looking at pornography, I seemed to calm down and actually hear what people were saying to me. My pastor explained that when we know a message or image is wrong and we continue to go back to it, it has become a god in our lives. I kind of thought he was old-fashioned and off his rocker at first. I still would have claimed God was first in my life, even though I knew what I was doing was wrong. But then my pastor said point-blank, "If God and this pornography were right before you, it is like you're saying 'sorry dude' to God and picking up the pornography." This helped me to see that I'd removed myself from His lordship and started making myself God, as though I knew what would truly benefit me and what would hurt me.

When my pastor further challenged me, I recognized that I had started looking at the girls at school differently. I would "mentally undress" them instead of seeing them as people created in God's image whose bodies are temples. Because I did that, I was already disrespecting my future wife. I had created a habit of doing things in secret . . . and I'd gotten pretty good at it.

Even though I thought I was just "being a teenager" and it wasn't a big deal, I came to realize that it was a HUGE deal. This behavior was defining me, and the more time had elapsed, the further entrenched in the sin of pornography I'd become. I want to be better than that. I want God to be proud of me when He sees the choices I'm making. Literally every time I pick up a book or select music or turn on my Xbox, I hear my pastor's voice saying, "Is this what God wants for you, or is this what you want for yourself?" Being honest and withstanding the temptation have lifted the weight of the world off my shoulders, and I am actually proud of the person I'm becoming. I'm living out my faith rather than spouting words, and I'm glorifying God in the process. That brings true pleasure!

Comment On This · Love This · Share with Friends

 Pam: Josh, I'm so sorry for the struggles you've walked through, but praise God for your parents and pastor helping you to recognize the choice/character relationship so that you can hold your head up high! To realize this while you are young and your character is being formed is a gift.

Comment On This · Love This · Share with Friends

📝 **Note: Character Like Clay.** "It is well for the world that in most of us, by the age of thirty, the character has set like plaster, and will never soften again" (William James). What do you think when you read these words? My initial reaction was panic! Really? Character can be "set" like plaster or cement? I could reach a point where I am no longer pliable? Although with God all things are possible, I think this is a sobering reminder that our early years are when we are being FORMED—MOLDED like clay.

If my character is being "molded" like clay on the potter's wheel, then I want to KNOW whose hands my character is being molded by! Is Jesus the potter of my character or is the WORLD? (Hollywood? Friends? My social network?) Who is in charge of the finished product that will be ME when I approach 30? Maybe we should be more INTENTIONAL about who it is we allow to mold us!

Kate: Cool (and scary) post! I haven't really fallen into any social media traps yet, but I know I need to stay on my guard. I'm a Christian, and to have His Word running through my head will help me fight any temptation that may come my way. Any verses you recommend?

Comment On This · Love This · Share with Friends

Pam: AWESOME idea! Here are some great Scriptures:

Then make my joy complete by being like-minded, having the same love, being one in spirit and of one mind (Philippians 2:2).

If you love me, keep my commands (John 14:15).

Not everyone who says to me, "Lord, Lord," will enter the kingdom of heaven, but only the one who does the will of my Father who is in heaven (Matthew 7:21).

But because of your stubbornness and your unrepentant heart, you are storing up wrath against yourself for the day of God's wrath, when his righteous judgment will be revealed. God "will repay each person according to what they have done." To those who by persistence in doing good seek glory, honor and immortality, he will give eternal life. But for those who are self-seeking and who reject the truth and follow evil, there will be wrath and anger (Romans 2:5-8).

Flee the evil desires of youth and pursue righteousness, faith, love and peace, along with those who call on the Lord out of a pure heart (2 Timothy 2:22).

I hope this helps, and I wish you the best!

Comment On This · Love This · Share with Friends

Pam: NOW is the time to be UNDER THE INFLUENCE of God and His Word, and to break free from the influence of ANYTHING or ANYONE that does not bring us closer to Jesus!

Comment On This · Love This · Share with Friends

Chapter 2

Hollywood Serves Up Junk

 Pam: Your perception of love might be influenced by the DVDs you were watching when you were a preschooler!

Comment On This · Love This · Share with Friends

 Jack: What in the world are you talking about?

Comment On This · Love This · Share with Friends

Pam: Our minds are influenced by story. Children who have barely graduated from sippy cups are getting ideas about love and marriage from Disney movies in which comatose girls awake to "heroes" who have never met them before! Realistic? Hardly. Powerful? Absolutely.

Comment On This · Love This · Share with Friends

 Laura: It would sure make relationships a whole lot easier if it worked that way! I want my prince charming to ride in and save me from the dating nightmare!

Comment On This · Love This · Share with Friends

 Daniel: Except that it isn't really love, nor is it a real relationship. Too often the big screen tells us that we can be fulfilled through first-time meetings and random hookups. Personally I'd rather invest my energy in making sure I'm becoming the person God wants ME to be. I kind of think focusing on personal character is the most important thing to finding the perfect mate. Don't you?

Comment On This · Love This · Share with Friends

> 📝 **Note: Life Is Not a Disney Fairy Tale.** It is painful to admit this, but Disney completely warped my perception of relationships. From the time I was young, I wanted to be Snow White or Cinderella. Well, mostly Snow White. She seemed to be the only princess who wasn't blonde! I dreamed of being the "fairest of them all" and making the wicked queen jealous. I imagined being worshipped by dwarfs named Happy and Sleepy and Dopey and Doc. What's more, even though my singing voice was painful to my own ears, I sincerely believed that if I were the fairest of them all, animals would come and sit by the window to eat out of my hands while I serenaded them.

Girls, wouldn't it be amazing if the only thing you had to do to catch the handsome prince was to eat an apple that would make you sleep (perhaps one laced with Advil® PM) and wait for him to ride up, fall in love with you (primarily because he couldn't hear your singing) and kiss you on the lips? Then, the two of you would ride off into the sunset.

Guys, wouldn't life feel simple if your parents could just host a dance and EVERY girl in the area would put on their best gowns to dance with you? Without even speaking words to one another, you would just know she is "the one," and not only would your life feel complete, but you would also be her HERO, rescuing her from her everyday existence. Talk about feeling wanted and "macho"!

However, Disney never finished the story. We never saw the relationship. All we ever got was the (alleged) "happily ever after." I was ripped off!

While you would think that we would grow out of our little childhood fantasies, join the real world, and mature in our ability to deal with relationships with the opposite sex, the truth is, most of us are still waiting for the glass slipper to fall off at the dance when the clock strikes midnight. As young women, we think that if we look pretty enough and have enough magic mice to create the perfect prom dress, we too will meet our princes and live happily ever after. Young men want the ego boost of fulfilling some girl's every dream. We need a wake-up call!

Here is the bottom line: Girls, if you want a man of God, you have to be a woman of God! Boys, if you want a God-honoring wife, you must honor God with your life right now. If you want respect, you have to be someone who is respectful. If you want honesty, you have to be honest. If you want kindness, you have to be kind. To have a successful relationship and future, the key is spending time NOW developing your own character.

Perhaps you find yourself saying, "Why do I always attract the losers?" If that is the case, maybe it's time for some real INNER SOUL SEARCHING. Rather than looking out, maybe it is time to look IN! What are you watching? How are you acting towards others? What do you believe?

Is that a lot of work? Yes it is. Maybe you wish you could just go back to the magic mirror, glass slippers or horse to ride in on and save the day. But, I promise, if you will do the WORK of growing up and maturing past the beautified gown and hero complex, your REAL, God-given spouse will be so much better than the fake, plastic one that cannot see the YOU behind the mask! You are a child of the King—loved beyond measure—so let's raise our standards high and spend a little more time on the INSIDE and less on the outside!

Aubrey: LOL. I've never thought about it like this, but you're totally right on.

Comment On This · Love This · Share with Friends

Paige: It is funny how we spend so much time looking for the "perfect" someone to date and completely gloss over who we are in the process.

Comment On This · Love This · Share with Friends

Tommy: Admittedly, I want to be the perfect, studly guy for whomever I date. I guess I need to think a little more about what makes me the "perfect" guy. It's a good time for me to ask, "Mirror, mirror, on the wall, am I focusing on the right things after all?"

Comment On This · Love This · Share with Friends

 Pam: "In the United States, the consumption of entertainment is almost like breathing. Yet how many of us consider that most entertainment is created to advance an agenda and deliver a message?" (Dick Rolfe)[1]

Comment On This · Love This · Share with Friends

 Jason: What do you think of one of the most popular movies in 2011, *No Strings Attached*?

Comment On This · Love This · Share with Friends

 Pam: First, let me say that it doesn't surprise me that a movie starring Ashton Kutcher would be successful. The man currently has over 6 million Twitter followers. That is more people than the entire population of Ireland! Obviously he is a popular, influential star.

However, the tagline, "Can sex friends stay best friends?" SHOULD make it pretty clear that the film doesn't follow a healthy order of intimacy. When we are asking, "Do meaningless hookups hurt friendships?" there is a BIG problem. The movie transports its viewers to another world and then challenges them to accept the wrong context for sex. Sex was not created for friendship or dates or even love. Sex was created for marriage—permanent commitment. Outside of that context, physical, emotional and spiritual consequences are an inevitable reality regardless of what Hollywood says.

Furthermore, *No Strings Attached* has been promoted as a date movie. Can a person really expect to attend a film with excessive nudity and obvious sex and then leave with the person he or she is attracted to in real life without being enticed? Not only is the film asking the wrong question, but it is also tempting the wrong people to act on what they have seen. Sadly, this can and WILL lead to pain.

Comment On This · Love This · Share with Friends

 Jason: That was my concern. It seems that the film promotes having sex first and then thinking through whether or not it was right later. I've seen your talk! I know having a strong understanding of boundaries FIRST is critical to making healthy choices later!

Comment On This · Love This · Share with Friends

Brittany: If you haven't seen the movie, don't. I don't even know why I watched it. It was nothing more than a booty call. Sex buddies. The message was "come and get it when you want it," and I found it disgusting. There were funny parts—I'm not going to lie—but it is because of movies like this that sex is viewed as a no-strings-attached act rather than something that is supposed to be only between husband and wife.

Comment On This · Love This · Share with Friends

Newsflash: 70% of respondents in one poll stated that "the amount of sex, violence and profanity in films bothers them."[2]

Sandra: I'm 15 and my best friend is 18. We have a great relationship. I want to talk to him about how serious I want our relationship to be, and how much I want to take our relationship to the next level. I mean, I love him. I know you're wondering if we've had sex and yes, we have. He's the best-best friend a girl could have, so I don't want to mess that up. What should I do?

Comment On This · Love This · Share with Friends

Pam: I am glad that you wrote me. It is important that you take time to seriously think this through. First of all, you are 15 having sex with an 18-year-old that you think is your "best friend." I don't know any 18-year-old boys who spend every day and night hanging out with freshman girls because they genuinely care about them. He's hanging out with you because he can't get a girl his own age to touch him with a 10-foot pole. I'm afraid your "best friend" is using all the right words to use you!

The reason you feel so strongly about this boy is that you have chemically bonded with him. When you had sex with this "best friend," your body released oxytocin, known as the "love hormone." Not only does oxytocin increase the level of trust you have for the person you're having intercourse with, but it also bonds you involuntarily to him, thereby increasing your desire to be with him.[3] This makes no-strings-attached sex IMPOSSIBLE, alters your ability to think clearly, and makes you unhealthy partners for each other.

You do need to talk to this boy. First of all, you need to tell him that this "too much too soon" relationship needs to end. It's not healthy in a friendship and it CERTAINLY isn't the way to approach a relationship. Then, tell him that you are going to see a doctor and get tested for sexually transmitted diseases (STDs), and you would encourage him to do the same.

I always suggest waiting to date until you are at least 16, and then dating in groups through the rest of high school. Please stay away from one-on-one situations with boys right now and BE the kind of person that you want to marry someday. Take time to build your character and set a NO GENITAL CONTACT until marriage boundary when you do decide to jump into the dating scene again.

Comment On This · Love This · Share with Friends

💔 Marti's Story

Movies are so powerful, especially with youth—including me. I remember seeing movies like *Dirty Dancing* and "realizing" that if I just followed my heart and made love when it really felt right (no matter what other people thought), things would turn out okay. Not the best decision to make at 15 . . . or 17! Even movies that people claim are great, like *Eternal Sunshine of the Spotless Mind*, really affected me. In that movie, the main message is that even if you aren't the best match, love is enough—you should always give "love" a chance. But nobody ever defined love! So it was just feelings—and I couldn't get over feeling that I was in love with my abusive boyfriend, and that love just had to be enough. The movie *Closer* focused on how messed up relationships are, and if they are really worth it—giving me the impression that everyone's relationships are totally screwed up. I figured if all relationships are complicated—involving cheating, lies, sex and whatever else—then mine was normal. All of these movies seem to have the same message: "Relationships are messy, and maybe they don't make sense, but if you love the person, you have to keep trying."

That was dangerous for me; the films' messages gave me an unhealthy concept of love. I dated my boyfriend for six years, constantly putting up with the physical, verbal and mental abuse, because I thought "but we love each other" and because I was so frightened to leave the only man I had ever had sex with.

Life really changed when I made some new friends. This group of friends encouraged me to have a different set of values, and to reinforce those values by the movies I watched. I stopped watching movies that encouraged dangerous behaviors, and instead chose movies that showed me how wonderful life can be when lived courageously and virtuously. I really enjoyed the movie *Bella*, and the movie about St. Thérèse always makes me want to live a better life. The movie *Arranged* shows how women can be true to their faith but still live in the modern world; I even loved the western *Open Range* because it focused on living with honor and respect. I also loved *The King's Speech* and *The Blind Side*, so current movies aren't totally out.

I just have to be careful what I watch, because the people who make those movies don't care about me; I'm a consumer to them. All they want to do is sell me a lifestyle that I already know is dangerous and harmful to my health and my heart. Movies that encourage degrading conduct and poor life choices are rampant, and people completely ignore the effect they have on the way we think.

There is a reason that propaganda is produced in video form: There is no filter for video. Unlike books, you can't set movies down to give yourself time to think and come back; you can't circle the words used. There aren't readily available bios about films' writers and producers that might tell you where they're coming from personally. You just have to swallow the message whole . . . and that's not the way I want messages to be put in my head.

Pam: Every day I interact with teenagers experiencing pregnancies they didn't plan. It's a life changer. Knowing that, I'm curious to know what you thought of *Juno.*

Comment On This · Love This · Share with Friends

Theresa: I didn't like the nonchalant attitude Juno had about her whole pregnancy. I liked the choice she made about the baby, but it seemed for them that sex was like, "whatever."

Comment On This · Love This · Share with Friends

Alex: When the main character says something like, "I got bored and had sex with you, and didn't want to, like, marry you," that is about as "whatever" as you can be. I felt bad that they didn't act like sex had any more value than something to do when you are bored. Sadly, my friends in the locker room who have sex treat it about the same way. They have no intentions of marrying their girlfriends. They are just using them for temporary entertainment and a good story.

Comment On This · Love This · Share with Friends

Tessa: Juno did show a lot of bravery in carrying the baby to term and then placing her in an adoptive home. Teens don't see or hear enough about adoption. It almost seems taboo, like, "I got myself into this mess and now I'm going to take care of it." They forget that adoption is a mature way to handle an immature decision. Seeing that promoted on the big screen was good.

Comment On This · Love This · Share with Friends

Todd: I liked that it seemed prolife. When Juno was looking into abortion, there was that girl there that talked about the baby having fingernails and stuff. I know they made her look like a nerd, but hearing the truth about early fetal development had to make some people think.

My girlfriend got pregnant last year. We totally weren't ready for a baby and freaked out. Like Juno, we didn't feel like marrying. Our parents are Christians who thought we would never have sex outside of marriage. Imagining how upset and disappointed they would be in us—along with the truth being made known to all of our friends—was just too much to deal with. Abortion seemed like our only answer. We rationalized it by telling ourselves that she was "early."

In a panic, I looked up a crisis pregnancy center for my girlfriend on the computer. They sounded like the type of place to do the procedure or whatever needed to happen. When I called the number, a very nice lady said they would set up a free appointment to go through information first. She also offered an ultrasound to see how far along Jenna (my girlfriend) was. We went the next day, and it wasn't the place I expected. Today I thank God for that. They didn't do the procedure, although they never pretended that they would. They said they would give us information and do the ultrasound. Well, I had no idea that abortion posed any risk to Jenna's body, or that this baby already had a heartbeat and brain waves.

The ultrasound was incredible. Jenna was six weeks along, and there was an obvious heartbeat. How could we minimize that? We cried and panicked some more. Then we decided that we had to tell our parents. It was tough.

I don't like that they made the baby development girl a dork, but I'm thankful more teens could think a little more about that like we were forced to. Life begins at conception. Too many young people don't recognize that. Obviously the pregnancy was hard. It wasn't as easy as the movie portrayed—on our relationship or on Jenna at school—but it is survivable, and the film did show that.

Comment On This · Love This · Share with Friends

 Ian: Wow, man. Your story makes me think a little more about my own actions. It was good that the movie showed some consequences, because we don't really see that very often.

Comment On This · Love This · Share with Friends

 Avery: I was only 13 when I saw the movie. They kind of acted like condoms would have made it better. Is that true?

Comment On This · Love This · Share with Friends

 Pam: GOOD QUESTION! Sadly, people are willing to trust a tiny piece of latex without knowing the truth. Here's the deal: Condoms fail in preventing pregnancy 15% of the time,[4] meaning one in six couples using them for birth control will experience a positive pregnancy test they never thought they would. Would you consider the brakes in your car safe if they failed you that often? Besides, that statistic is just with regards to pregnancy. Condoms fail in stopping the spread of STDs, too. The ONLY safe choice is NO GENITAL CONTACT outside of marriage!

Comment On This · Love This · Share with Friends

❣ Liza's Story

I saw your post about Juno and had to write you. I loved that she wanted to find the right, loving parents for her baby, but I struggled when she said, "In thirty-odd weeks we can just pretend that this never happened." Nothing could be further from the truth.

I got pregnant with a little boy when I was 15. At first I thought it would be fun to have a baby to love, but then I realized that parenting is the biggest job of all, and I just wasn't ready for that yet. We'd discussed abortion in school, and I couldn't kill an innocent baby either.

It was really hard. My parents had me talk to a counselor weekly. I decided on adoption so that this boy could have the parents he deserved. But I was scared, nervous and in pain. Pain described my life. I would tear up thinking about my delivery day coming, and then my baby being gone in a matter of seconds. I was attached to that little guy inside of me. How could I let him go?

I wanted to see what he looked like, so I chose an open adoption. I'm so thankful I did. I broke up with my boyfriend a few days after the birth, and that plunged me into a dark hole for a while. There was so much transition. It isn't as easy as just handing the baby off and then going on with your life, strumming the guitar and singing with your man—everything about your world changes. I continued seeing a counselor for many, many months. I knew that the decision I made for my son was the right and most loving one, but my heart didn't believe it at first.

I'm thankful the movie encouraged adoption, but I pray people will recognize the true emotional challenge that comes with this beautiful choice. To walk into it thinking you can pretend it away after delivery is a complete falsehood.

Pam: "Cinema is the most beautiful fraud in the world" (Jean-Luc Godard).

Comment On This · Love This · Share with Friends

Adrian: Sometimes I probably don't think enough about the deceit movies present. Oftentimes I just go because they are filling some kind of void in my life.

Comment On This · Love This · Share with Friends

Erin: Good point. I'm addicted to the *Twilight* movies and books. I wish my life had that much adventure in it.

Comment On This · Love This · Share with Friends

 Rebecca: I like how love is always a major commitment that is taken very seriously. I don't think that is deceitful.

Comment On This · Love This · Share with Friends

 Caryn: I agree. I think the series portrays relationships very well. Edward is "old fashioned" and is absolutely adamant about waiting to have sex until they are married, which is something you never see in popular films today.

Comment On This · Love This · Share with Friends

 Jenny: They don't wait to have sex because it's wrong outside of marriage, guys! They wait because of the danger. There were some aspects about it that kind of freaked me out. I mean, Bella thinks Edward is such a hero, and because she thinks that, she is always trying to please him. That seems unhealthy. Also, what is up with him watching her sleep before he introduces himself? Creepy!

Comment On This · Love This · Share with Friends

📝 **Note: Escaping the Vampire.** Since you all brought up so much discussion about *Twilight*, I wanted to share this note from my friend, Kimberly Powers. She recently wrote *Escaping the Vampire*,[5] and I know you'll be intrigued by what she has to say!

I was caught off guard. A bit surprised by his alluring charm, it was only after several scenes that the "idea of Edward the vampire" had grabbed my heart as well. I found myself in many ways right there emotionally with Bella.

Good girls attracted to bad boys is an old story. We can track it for centuries. The promise of excitement and the allure of danger is so very appealing, especially if there is a chance for a happily ever after. . . .

As I watched *Twilight*, I waited tensely for a devious dark villain to appear. But he never showed up—at least, not in the way I expected. Instead, I watched Edward, an intriguingly handsome modern dark knight, sweep the heroine, Bella, off her feet. He appeared as a noble character, desperate to love and be loved.

We are enthralled by the idea of our very own Edward. But imagine that this iconic, hunky, bad-boy hero "Edward type" could be outdone so easily by an eternally loving, fiercely protective Savior. Pretty cool thought.

Stop for a moment and take this in: You are free to stop filling your empty spaces inside with lesser things, with less than God's love. Many girls have shared their own disillusion with their search for a story of epic love. Maybe this is your story. Maybe you find yourself consumed by life-sucking lies and you need a rescue. Maybe you find yourself in the midst of so much "yuck" and feel unworthy of His love. I have REALLY good news. There is a true epic love story—far beyond fantasy. When you have experienced this type of undying love . . . nothing else compares.

At the core of every one of our hearts is a longing to be truly, madly and deeply loved. But stop and think on this one. No mortal, not even Edward, can offer a perfect, eternal, unconditionally loving relationship—the one we so long for. So why do our hearts keep longing so hard after something we can never find—something that simply does not exist? Unless it does. Unless this longing is a hunger for what our souls were created for. What if our souls were shaped for Someone? Someone amazing, who is incredibly attentive to our every need and who experiences life with us.

About three things you can be absolutely positive: First, every girl longs to be loved with a vast and endless passion. Second, there is a fiercely protective Immortal Hero who longs for your heart. And third, He loves you with an unconditional and irrevocable love.

This epic love story—one even greater than the story of Bella and Edward—has already been written, with you in mind as the beautiful heroine. Only this is no fantasy. You can live your life eternally with the Immortal Hero who cherishes everything about you, protects you, and loves you more deeply than you could ever imagine."

 Pam: There have been some great films in recent years that have not only entertained me but also helped influence the world positively. THIS makes me thankful for cinema!

Comment On This · Love This · Share with Friends

 Ben: I loved *The Lion, the Witch, and the Wardrobe.* There was so much power in Lucy's words about Aslan (who represented Christ). When Mr. Tumnus said, "He's not a tame lion," and she responded, "No, but he is good," it brought a smile to my face.

Comment On This · Love This · Share with Friends

 Haddie: I remember going to *The Passion of the Christ* and weeping in my seat when they beat Him before the crucifixion. Seriously, I wanted to scream, "ENOUGH!" And yet, to have that visual of His personal love for me was so meaningful.

Comment On This · Love This · Share with Friends

Jared: *To Save a Life* has my wheels spinning. What do I want my life to be about? What I do matters. I could be the one to make a LIFE-SAVING difference in someone's life!
Comment On This · Love This · Share with Friends

Rachel: One of my faves is *A Walk to Remember.* If you study movies carefully, you'll see that the movies where two people do NOT have sex while dating always have a more intense romance. You always want those couples to stay together. When they are sexually active, ESPECIALLY early on in the dating game, the movie is more of a comedy than a heated and pure romance. I want something that is real, not fake, in my life.
Comment On This · Love This · Share with Friends

Pam: Great examples! Recently, I had the privilege to see an advance viewing of *Courageous.* I LOVED the way this film encouraged men to be good fathers and leaders in their homes. A scene where one of the fathers takes his 15-year-old daughter to dinner, tells her how special she is to him and to God, and encourages her to save herself for her future husband was incredibly powerful! What a great example of how film can model GOOD behavior and help encourage us.
Comment On This · Love This · Share with Friends

Shayna: Hey, Pam! I just saw the movie *Precious.* Even though I felt helpless when I watched it, I think it's a good film to see. Sexual abuse is a real problem in our society, but I've never seen it personally played out. Watching the movie helped me to better understand the intense pain that sexual assault survivors feel. One person's choice to hurt another— their sin—has incredible impact. Have you seen it? Do you agree that this influences the world positively? Some people think I'm crazy!
Comment On This · Love This · Share with Friends

Pam: Yes, I have seen it. While it was painful to watch, you spoke well of its valuable message.
Comment On This · Love This · Share with Friends

Dave: I've heard of this movie but have no clue what it is about. Can somebody fill me in?
Comment On This · Love This · Share with Friends

Pam: Dave, the film is set in Harlem in the late 1980s. Claireece Precious Jones is the main character. Although she is only 16, she is dealing with more pain than any one person should have to endure. Her parents aren't fit, to say the least. Precious's mother physically and emotionally abuses her, and her father is a drug addict who impregnates her. As if that kind of pregnancy would not be hard enough to deal with, Precious's school threatens to expel her. She transfers to a new school where loving adults help Precious deal with the emotional pain caused by the abuse.

I don't want to give too much away, so I'll just say that the movie brilliantly deals with real-life themes that many around us have buried deep within themselves. It also shows how sin ruins the life of the sinner and also harms innocent people who end up being terribly damaged by their sinful behavior.

Comment On This · Love This · Share with Friends

Bo: Even though most of what I saw and heard in this movie made me sick, I'm glad I saw it, because I found myself intensely caring about Precious. It wasn't a "feel good" movie, but it inspired me to connect to a real-life issue I had been pretending away.

Comment On This · Love This · Share with Friends

Katrina: The part where Precious cries out, "Love ain't done nothing for me!" had me in tears. Precious feels angry, but I loved that by the end she has a new perspective on love and self-worth.

Comment On This · Love This · Share with Friends

Pam: Amen. The movie doesn't have a faith focus, and we haven't all been in Precious's shoes—thank God—but everyone has been hurt and angry. This film syncs with Christ's message to each of us in the midst of those emotions: We are valued, loved and totally precious to Him.

Comment On This · Love This · Share with Friends

> **@ Link:** If you are looking for a great resource to help you determine whether a movie is worth seeing or should be avoided, I encourage you to check out PLUGGED IN. The site has well-written, thorough reviews that will give you truthful information to help you decide if the film you're considering is a good way to spend your money and time! http://www.pluggedin.com/

Pam: A movie cannot change the world, but it CAN change the people who will change the world. Is your perception being positively or negatively influenced by what you're viewing?

Comment On This · Love This · Share with Friends

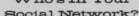
Chapter 3

Jersey Shore, Teen Mom Serving a Steady Diet of Big Macs

Pam: Why is it that whenever I turn on my TV, I struggle to find something worthy of watching?

Comment On This · Love This · Share with Friends

Lina: As an abstinence educator, I'm just wondering what you think of *Teen Mom*?

Comment On This · Love This · Share with Friends

Pam: Good question! Let me start by saying that I am THANKFUL all of these girls chose life. They were in the position of having to decide if their unborn children would see the light of day, and they chose LIFE and not death.

As an adopted child, I am a big proponent of adoption. When a girl chooses to parent, she has tremendous odds stacked against her. Fewer than a third of parents who begin their families before age 18 will graduate from high school,[1] and because of that, 64 percent of teen-parented children will grow up in poverty.[2] Relationships are also likely to fail. In fact, 80 percent of teen fathers won't marry their children's mothers.[3] This environment is not one that often promotes healthy parents or thriving children.

Because this show turns everyday teens into reality television stars, they transition from struggling teen to celebrity status overnight. Not only are they all over magazine covers and calendars, walking the red carpet and making appearances on other shows, but they are also being paid VERY WELL to allow cameras into their lives. In fact, these "stars" are getting paid $60,000-$65,000 per season![4] That salary offers a posh lifestyle that many well-educated adults don't have—let alone the average teen mom who might be trying to make ends meet with night shifts at Burger King. Hardly reality!

Since many teens know this, there is concern that girls are trying to get pregnant in order to become the newest reality star.

After all, some of the current teen moms are aging. In fact, Amber Portman is now 20, no longer fitting the age demographic. With 3 in 10 teens in the United States getting pregnant before the age of 20,[5] competition, sadly, runs high. Most pregnant 16-year-olds will not make the cut for *16 and Pregnant* (the predecessor to *Teen Mom*). This leaves a lot of mothers AND THEIR BABIES on their own.

Beyond the concern about attempted teen pregnancy, I am troubled by how the show characterizes life. Are there going to be teen moms? Absolutely. However, the goal should be to educate teen parents who now recognize that another life is dependent on them so that they will make wise decisions for the benefit of their babies (and themselves). That has not been the case around this show.

Cohabitation is a well-known set-up for divorce. Couples who marry after living together are 50 percent more likely to divorce than couples who do not—and that is for the couples that actually make it to the altar. A shocking 45 percent of couples "preparing for marriage" will never marry.[6] Yet one of the mothers on *Teen Mom 2* discussed her decision to move in with her boyfriend. As if that is not bad enough, this came only a few weeks after the couple broke up and then got back together. Interestingly, in this fast-forward approach to life, the couple married after just a few months of living together. I know that these young people want to right their wrong, but they haven't built their relationship on healthy choices—and that sets them up for massive failure. It would be more helpful to show couples trying to make it work by living apart, practicing recycled virginity, and going through solid premarital counseling to increase their chances for a successful marriage—for the sake of the young parents and their babies.

Another concern is that news surrounding the show does not promote a healthy sense of respect for the body. Recently, one of the moms modeled in a racy calendar photo. For this teen mom to continue seeking attention and worth by flashing her skin before the camera promotes a cycle of dangerous choices. As a culture, we need to be helping teenagers who have chosen sex outside of marriage in the past to realize that their bodies do not define their value. For these reasons and more, I am concerned about *Teen Mom* and the messages it is sending.

Comment On This · Love This · Share with Friends

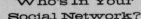
Jersey Shore, Teen Mom Serving a Steady Diet of Big Macs

Jamie: I think *Teen Mom* was initially a good concept, because it shows how difficult it is to raise babies as a teen. However, people are getting the wrong message from it, and it almost glorifies teen pregnancy.

Comment On This · Love This · Share with Friends

Rosanne: I think *Teen Mom* deals mostly with reality, but I have to agree with Jamie. It does glorify teen pregnancy.

Comment On This · Love This · Share with Friends

Debbie: I've watched the show on occasion, and I think it is definitely scripted. I admired the couple in the first season that placed their baby for adoption and the others that are trying to make things work. There are real emotions involved. But the whole voice-over/narrator thing is what keeps it from being reality.

Comment On This · Love This · Share with Friends

Tonya: I am a teen mom, and it is really hard. That is why I am so thankful for Pam's message. This show does not show it all: the gazillion diaper changes, the sleepless nights, the struggle to get homework done—all the things that are "routine" and not entertainment, so they get cut, and yet they're the things that make parenting really difficult. Most of us aren't having little spats with our mom in the kitchen and then going out for ice cream on a date to talk about our next modeling job. We are in sweats . . . on the verge of tears . . . doing everything in our power to do what is right and responsible so that little crying person has a good life.

Comment On This · Love This · Share with Friends

📝 **Note: Stop Exploiting Teen Pregnancy.** I loved this very honest blog reflection from a teen mom, Cassie Boorn, about *Teen Mom*. They are some wonderful words to think through!

There has been a ton of talk and hype about this quite popular show *Teen Mom*. I have not watched the show and I really never plan to.

I really hate talking about these things because I am partial. I had a child at 18.

Being a young mom is a lot of work. Not only do you have a new child to take care of but a journey to figure out who you are and who this person you are raising your child with is. It is a struggle and a dance that takes many years to perfect. Understanding the complexities of love and relationships. Making peace with the guilt that motherhood inevitably brings and coming to terms with who you are and this life that you are living. Being a young mother takes the journey of being a young girl and makes it so much more complex that you are lucky if you can wade through it successfully. You are lucky if you have a support team strong enough to pull you through.

Being a young mother is hard.

It is very easy to focus on the struggle that is being a young mother. The poor decisions that were made that got you there. The mistakes you should have thought through a little more and the sin that rides on your shoulders.

When I was pregnant with Aiden, I was never met with a congratulations. I never expected one. However, I didn't expect the mass number of strangers who would give me the "you know how you got that way" talk. And the first time I was asked for parenting advice? Aiden was well over a year old and I still remember the feeling I got that day. The realization that not only was I a mother but a mother worthy of sharing advice about parenting.

I am not saying that we should promote young motherhood.

I am saying that we should stop exploiting it.

When a young mother succeeds? People are shocked.

As a society. As women. As humans capable of making mistakes. We have to stop focusing on the tragedy of having babies too young and start focusing on supporting and building up the young girls that had a baby too young.[7]

Kirsten: Amen. Creating a family "backward" from God's design certainly creates extra hurdles, but as a culture we need to stop "enjoying" the difficulty caused by wrong choices and help raise these young people to a higher standard. In our crisis pregnancy center, we offer parenting courses, relationship counseling and other tools to help people in difficult situations achieve success. This is where our focus should lie. It is my hope that any struggling young person will call 1-800-395-HELP so they too can move their lives forward rather than remain stuck in a rut.

Comment On This · Love This · Share with Friends

@ Link: If you are a teen mom, please check out www.standupgirl.com for further encouragement. With determination, faith and a willingness to let people mentor you, you CAN achieve the best for both you and your baby.

Pam: The problem with reality television is that they are portraying relationships that don't always jive with reality.

Comment On This · Love This · Share with Friends

Paul: Do you think too much emphasis is placed on what people watch and not enough on how they actually live?

Comment On This · Love This · Share with Friends

Amanda: *Jersey Shore* is one of my favorite shows on TV right now. It's so entertaining. I know it might not be completely realistic, but then again, TV IS what we use to escape reality.
Comment On This · Love This · Share with Friends

 Pam: Let's just praise God that you recognize that it isn't realistic. I laughed when a review in *Plugged In* said, "Watching it made me want to take antibiotics to ward off whatever infections were being pumped through my flat screen."[8] I can only imagine the number of STDs being shared among that cast!
Comment On This · Love This · Share with Friends

 Holly: Amanda, don't be too quick to assume that people don't use *Jersey Shore* for relationship advice. I know tons of people model their behavior on what they see on that show.
Comment On This · Love This · Share with Friends

 Pam: Regardless of whether people think they are or not, they ARE being influenced by these unhealthy depictions. You simply CANNOT put ideas into your brain without having them make an impression on your view of God's standards and the world around you. Over time, they will corrode your faith and values and change you from the inside out.
Comment On This · Love This · Share with Friends

 Adam: I'm just going to lay out all the cards. I am not close to my parents. We've never talked about sex, and it feels awkward to bring it up now. We've dabbled in and out of churches, but going each week is not a priority to my parents, and therefore it isn't to me either. I have to get relationship help from somewhere. I don't want to be the guy that asks the girl out and then looks like a dork because I don't know how to act or what to say. I do watch *Jersey Shore* and *Skins* for ideas. *Skins* is especially helpful because it is about teens. Even the actors are teens. I don't know what else to do.
Comment On This · Love This · Share with Friends

 Pam: First of all, let me apologize for the lack of adult communication in your life. As parents, it is our responsibility to share the truth with our children and other young people in our lives, so that you can make wise choices.

Both *Jersey Shore* and *Skins* are spoon-feeding you lies, not the truth about most people and relationships in real life. If you let me, I would love to share some insight that will help you be a more desirable date.

Most important for you to know is that a little over one-third of all high school students are actually having sex.[9] Despite the impression that everyone wants and is having sex, MORE students desire relationships of integrity and are waiting. If you want to show a girl that you care about her, you have to communicate to her through your actions and requests that she is more than the next notch on your belt. You have to show her that you respect her and are drawn to her heart, not her physical features. To do this, you must set a NO GENITAL CONTACT boundary on the first date. Then, stay in public settings and go to activities and events you mutually enjoy. This will help you get to know each other better in a healthy way.

Although *Skins* suggests it is "normal" for teenage boys to have sex with anyone willing, and *Jersey Shore* tells you it is fine to lather lotion on practically nude girls on the beach and cheat on your girlfriend, men of character recognize that each of these girls is someone's future wife and deserves to be honored. Truly normal boys have brains that supersede raging hormones. If they don't, they will pay. You cannot have sex outside of marriage without suffering consequences. Sexual partners are emotionally bonded with each other. When sex is treated as "meaningless fun," the strength of that bond decreases with every partner, leaving precious little meaningful intimacy for your future spouse. Physically, your chance of disease is EXTREMELY high. One in four of your classmates has at least one STD.[10] On any given day, 10,000 of your peers will find out they are infected—and that number doesn't include your classmates who aren't getting tested (which is most of them).[11]

Adam, I want you to travel with me a few years down the road. You've found the girl of your dreams and bought the perfect diamond. In the middle of the perfectly planned date, you pull out that ring and say, "Will you marry me? By the way, I have genital herpes. I watched a lot of *Skins* and *Jersey Shore* back in the day, and it turns out condoms don't mean safe sex after all. Sadly, you'll get herpes, too, and it may affect the delivery of our children and inflict massive pain on you, but please, marry me." What do you think she will say? Is that what you REALLY want to have to tell the woman you hope to marry on that day?

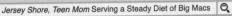
Adding to the lies is the representation of teen alcohol and drug use. Sixty-five percent of teens have not had a drink in the past month,[12] and only 10 percent of 12- to 17-year-olds are using illicit drugs.[13] For those who do use alcohol or drugs, the chances of making sexual choices they otherwise would not make skyrocket.

So, if you want to be in the statistically "in" crowd when it comes to sex, drugs and alcohol, DON'T DO IT. Adam, you were created by a God who loves you. I would strongly suggest that you find a church-attending friend to tag along with. Dig into God's Word and get a REAL picture of love. The Bible makes it very clear.

Comment On This · Love This · Share with Friends

Note: Reality TV ISN'T Reality. "I am mez-merized by a box that brightenz my room and cloudz my vizion" (Andrew Malekoff). It's Friday evening and you're gathered around the TV with your friends, talking about Snookie, Kim Kardashian, the Real Housewives of Orange County, Amber Portwood, Kendra and other household names.

In recent years, the number of "reality TV" shows has escalated to the point that approximately one in every four primetime TV programs falls into this category.[14] Based on their ridiculously successful ratings, society seems to be reaffirming to TV execs that we are all hungering to watch people with no acting skill or brain power do absolutely nothing. The execs must love this. After all, one hour of reality TV generally costs a few hundred thousand dollars to make, compared to the 1 to 3 million dollars needed to produce a scripted drama.[15]

We should be embarrassed. Have we really become the kind of people who just love to drown ourselves in the humiliation, terrible behavior, really bad choices and mental breakdowns of others? Has television become such an extension of the world we live in that we now gossip about these "stars" over lunch in the cafeteria as though they were our best friends?

The more sinister thing, I think, is that these shows purport to be REALITY, but are they? Read this poem by Andrew Malekoff:

reality tv is not really real: reality tv is a fairy tale

reality tv is not viewed in real time:
    is heavily edited
    highly contrived
    artificial
    staged and stilted
    two-dimensional
    black and white
    centralized
    commercialized
    homogenized.

reality tv promotes corporate culture:
  creates spectators rather than doers
  markets our young to advertisers
  sells their eyeballs to the highest bidder.

reality tv is wrapped in warped values:
  is obsessed with winning at all costs
  capitalizes on cruelty
  glorifies greed
  humiliates
  snoops
  bullies
  overpowers
  thrives on putdowns
  teaches our young not to trust.

reality tv exploits women and young girls:
  magnifies flaws
  says looks matter most
  celebrates surgical alteration
  institutionalizes eating disorders.

reality tv is a socially toxic:
  spiritual pollutant.

reality tv has no soul:
  only sponsors.

reality tv has no taste:
  is less filling.

reality tv is not really real:
  reality tv is a fairy tale.[16]

Some might argue that there have always been shows like this, but the sheer volume of today's reality shows, as well as the often jaw-dropping behavior of their stars, has opened a new chapter in a very old debate: Can what we see and hear on television affect us for the worse? I think taking a look at the students walking the hallways of your school will give you the answer!

Jed: These "everyday living" reality TV shows represent lowest-common-denominator television. They're revolting and offensive to my intelligence!

Comment On This · Love This · Share with Friends

46

Elyse: Sometimes I think people watch these shows to feel better about themselves. But measures of comparison are not what God is asking of me. As a Christian in today's world, I need to pray for the people on these shows, but then choose to watch the good stuff.

Comment On This · Love This · Share with Friends

Max: That's right. Bring on the sports!

Comment On This · Love This · Share with Friends

Pam: "All television is educational television. The question is: what is it teaching?" (Nicholas Johnson).

Comment On This · Love This · Share with Friends

Alisha: I watched the "Sexy" episode of *Glee* last night and was kind of confused. Holly had this "sharing circle" where people were encouraged to simply share feelings. The show gave the impression that it was okay to act on those feelings, no matter what they were. I know that isn't true. Sometimes what I want to do isn't the right thing to do.

Comment On This · Love This · Share with Friends

Pam: You're correct that this scenario sends the message that it is okay to act on our feelings at any given moment, but that IS NOT healthy in real life. We must act in the truth of God's Word— not according to our wishy-washy, come-and-go emotions that will lead us astray. Regret is a result of acting irresponsibly because of human emotions. Confidence is the result of following God's will.

Comment On This · Love This · Share with Friends

Janessa: Good advice. We are so bombarded by false representations of "normalcy" on TV that we sometimes lose sight of reality.

Comment On This · Love This · Share with Friends

☞ **Note: Why I'm Quitting the *Glee* Club.** I too saw the "Sexy" episode of *Glee* last night. Although I quit watching the show awhile back because I felt it made a mockery of my Christian faith, I wanted to see what Hollywood would have to preach in an episode obviously designed around the subject of my talk.

I was horrified. When Holly said that abstinence was not a realistic option for teens, I wanted to throw something at the TV screen on behalf of all of you who DO HAVE CHARACTER and ARE MAKING HEALTHY CHOICES. More of you are choosing abstinence than are not, and I want to encourage you to continue to STAND STRONG!

My friend Vicki Courtney wrote an amazing blog post about the value of your body when this subject was broached in an earlier episode. Please read this excerpt from "Why I'm Quitting the *Glee* club" and think about what she says:

> Then came the Britney Spears episode with the weathered theme that "bad is the new good." Wow, that's creative. Haven't we been down this road before? I found it ironic that the episode celebrated the girls-gone-wild movement Britney built her career upon, yet failed to tell the whole story. If they're going to have a moral to each episode, shouldn't they have reminded girls that Britney's stint in the girls-gone-wild club left her with a bald head, hospitalized on the verge of a nervous breakdown, and still to this day, under the conservatorship of her father? Not much to celebrate, if you ask me.
>
> This is where I'm left scratching my head in confusion. We are encouraged in previous episodes to love and respect people regardless of sexual orientation or religious beliefs, yet when it comes to respecting girls for the person they are, rather than the sum of their "sexy" parts, forget about it. Feminists ought to be screaming over this double standard. The sexualization and objectification of girls is damaging to their emotional and physical well-being. Where is that message? I'm weary of the double standard. Love everyone for who they are. Respect everyone for what they believe. Except, that is, young women who are nothing more than the sum of their parts.
>
> I had already given up the show when news hit of the controversial, near-naked schoolgirl photo shoot that *Glee* main characters Dianna Agron and Lea Michele recently participated in for *GQ* magazine. Why would two amazingly talented girls who have already built a reputation on talent, shed their clothes for a pervy photo shoot and cater to a narrow audience of men who enjoy fantasizing about hooking up with UNDER-AGED schoolgirls? I'll tell you why: They've bought into the very message their show peddled with the Britney episode. Like most other girls, they have been indoctrinated over the years to base their worth on the sum of their parts. My heart hurts for these two young women, who obviously lack true self-respect and as a result, somehow imagined that catcalls from *GQ* readers (and the perverts who are sure to come out of the woodwork) would feel better than accolades and applause for actual *talent*.
>
> The actresses' apparent need of male approval will come with a price. It will reinforce the message young girls are bombarded with daily: "It doesn't matter if you're smart or talented, you still have to know how to work it and please the guys. Give 'em what they want. Fulfill their fantasies . . . or at the very least, tease them into thinking you will." . . .
>
> A day will surely come when the sum of their parts won't measure up to the culture's narrow standard. For those who've based their worth on this faulty equation, the fallout won't be pretty.[17]

Vicki's insights are right on. There have been several episodes formed around the concept of love (which often gets reduced to sex) and, for whatever reason, males in the show are commonly shown pressuring the hyper-sexualized girls to put out. But ALL of our bodies—male and female—are to be treasured. In 1 Corinthians 6:20, Paul says, "You were bought at a price. Therefore honor God with your bodies." Even the Chastity Club's "It's the teasing not the pleasing" motto sends the wrong message. If you want a fun dating life, followed by a healthy marriage, you must look in the mirror and ask, "How can I act today to respect my body now and be a good spouse later?"

Thomas: I am a teenager who has watched the show numerous times and wishes I never had. The singing is good, but the obvious immorality isn't. Even if it is happening in real life, can't we keep it out of our programming?

Comment On This · Love This · Share with Friends

Lindsey: It sucks when TV feels the need to pick on those of us with good values and make us feel like we are stupid because of it.

Comment On This · Love This · Share with Friends

Connor: For me, the final straw was "Grilled Cheesus." To equate God to Santa and picture Him in a burned sandwich was offensive.

Comment On This · Love This · Share with Friends

Pam: When the show started, it was light humor and fun tunes. There didn't seem to be a political agenda. Many of us enjoyed it. Now, as the storylines seem to contain a persuasive agenda, it is important that we raise our guards and pray about whether or not it is something we should be watching.

Comment On This · Love This · Share with Friends

📰 **Newsflash:** "Underage female characters are shown participating in an even higher percentage of sexual situations than their adult counterparts: 47 percent to 29 percent respectively."[18]

Keri: When I was little, I was watching *Golden Girls* with my grandma, and the characters were talking about "safe sex" and how they were going to buy condoms for a cruise. My grandma probably thought I was so young I didn't know what they were talking about. But I remember to this day thinking, *Well, those nice old ladies are having sex and they're*

not married, so it must be okay. I became pregnant at 19, before marriage. We have now been married for eight years, and I am here to tell you that your abstinence message needs to be heard!

Comment On This · Love This · Share with Friends

 Pam: Thank you for the encouraging note. I praise God for how He has redeemed your life. I pray that all of you continue to listen to Him and tune out the lies of the world!

Comment On This · Love This · Share with Friends

🐾 Anthony's Story

 It all started for me when I was about five or six years old. I clearly remember being excused from the dinner table one evening and going into the living room to watch TV. I was flicking through the channels and—Bam!—right in front of me were two naked girls doing something on a workout bench. I am still shocked by how that image is burned into my brain. My father came over and turned off the TV, but that first taste of pornography left me wanting more.

Later, I maintained a steady diet of *Married with Children* and other shows like it. My parents thought it was funny. I recall watching it as a family on Sunday nights. But to me it was much more—I was mesmerized by Kelly and even Al's wife, Peggy. Al was constantly talking about porn and visiting strip clubs. Bud, his son, was always trying to "get some" from girls. The show was a half-hour of undiluted lust streamed directly into my brain. I remember getting aroused as a young boy watching this show. These kinds of programs became my life. I would tape them and watch them over and over, desperately trying to see a little more skin revealed.

My young heart and innocence were corrupted. I judged women by their looks; if they did nothing for me, I did not want to have anything to do with them. I made friends based on the attractiveness of their sisters and mothers. I can see clearly now how my addiction to this type of TV show destroyed my ability to see women as people.

The ONLY thought in my head was how I could get sex. What MTV started was a gold mine for me. I watched every video I could. Soon enough, this became boring as well. I would read the *TV Guide* every day to see if any adult movies would be on HBO or Cinemax or whatever channel. I would set my alarm and get up at crazy hours, secretly taping these shows so I could enjoy them when my parents left me home alone. I had no self-control. I was an animal, consuming all I could, whenever I could.

At 12 years old, I was an addict. I was in chains, but it would only get worse. Porn led to new friends with questionable morals, which led to smoking and drinking, which led to sex, drugs and rock and roll. I tried everything I could. I knew I had a problem when I was practically prostituting myself just to have sex. I was consumed with lust.

It wasn't until I dated a girl I'll call "Jess" that my life changed. She loved me. I hated her. But she was cute and innocent. I wanted to use her. And I did. Then I dumped her. Later, I heard she had tried to kill herself. For the first time in my life, I was faced with the reality of my lust. Someone almost died because of me! I was a jerk. I couldn't look at myself in the mirror. I did not enjoy sex the way I once did.

From there I started to pursue forgiveness. After a while, I stumbled into a church and went to confession. Now here I am, eight years later—a recovering porn addict whose problem started with inappropriate ideas on TV—with an awesome wife and five children. Today I am a Catholic evangelist who speaks at Diocesan conferences, parish groups and wherever else I am invited, and I'm also a leader of a men's group, trying to help others avoid the trap that once ensnared me.

 Pam: Perhaps one of the reasons people don't know how priceless they are is because we've lost a sense that everything comes with a price.
Comment On This · Love This · Share with Friends

 Theresa: This is a case of parents fostering poor attitudes. Have you seen *Outrageous Kid Parties* on TLC? Kids that are like six years old are getting $30,000 birthday parties! With this "the sky is the limit" approach, how can they have any sense of delayed gratification in life?
Comment On This · Love This · Share with Friends

 Pam: Good point! Delayed gratification is a learned skill from toddlerhood. When people throw cash around like confetti, the value of a hard-work ethic is lost, not to mention the glorified blatant disrespect of what God has given us.
Comment On This · Love This · Share with Friends

 Brit: Oh my gosh! You should watch *My Super Sweet 16*. It's a bunch of spoiled little brats who worship money. Seriously, it's a teenager's version of *Bridezilla!*
Comment On This · Love This · Share with Friends

 David: We live in an "it's all about me" culture, and as long as we continue to watch—even if it is to gawk and roll our eyes at what we see—we promote the message.
Comment On This · Love This · Share with Friends

📝 **Note: Money, Money, Money.** Perhaps blaming "money" is a bit simplistic. It's not the money that is really the problem. It is the greed, jealousy and "idol worship" that the LOVE of money brings. That's why the apostle Paul said in 1 Timothy 6:10, "For the love of money is the root of all kinds of evil. And some people, craving money, have wandered from the true faith and pierced themselves with many sorrows" (*NLT*).

Unfortunately, reality television has brought the "love of money" to new lows. With *My Super Sweet 16, Outrageous Kid Parties, Cribs* and other shows proudly displaying such hideous examples of spoiled brats, my 16-year-old simply asking for the latest PlayStation game appears angelic.

Perhaps we think that because others have such out-of-control gluttony and pride, we can feel better about our "minor" amounts of greed and want. The problem, however, is that the difference is only a matter of degree. Any belief that "stuff" (the latest video game, hot pair of jeans, car, iPad, phone, purse or whatever you "covet") will bring you happiness is damaging. Such an attitude leads to judging ourselves according to the materialistic standards of others. In an insidious race to "keep up with the Joneses," we dangerously begin to believe that our VALUE is based on what we OWN rather than on who we are in God!

Lydia: Are you surprised by what you see on TV? How do you think Christians should respond? It's so hard when it feels like that is all that is on!

Comment On This · Love This · Share with Friends

Pam: As Christians, we need to remember that it is okay to say no to watching TV. We don't have to have it on!

I am not surprised by what we see. We live in a fallen world. Whether we are dealing with sex or money, the flesh is drawn to the "gimme culture" that suggests we are entitled to whatever we want whenever we want it. However, as Christians, we can't indulge in the way of the flesh. Romans 13:13 comes to mind: "Let us behave decently, as in the daytime, not in carousing and drunkenness, not in sexual immorality and debauchery, not in dissension and jealousy." We are called to a higher standard.

Because the flesh will direct us towards heartache, we MUST always ask ourselves, "Is this show in line with God's teaching?" God created us to experience the truly fulfilled life through submission and patience. We aren't wild animals that can't control ourselves. We are human beings capable of exercising restraint and wisdom. In Galatians 6:7, Paul is very clear: "Do not be deceived: God cannot be mocked. A man reaps what he sows."

Comment On This · Love This · Share with Friends

Pam: Turn off what is bad, and welcome what is good. Stay away from watching sinful behavior not labeled as such. This will help you discern what is worthy of watching.

Comment On This · Love This · Share with Friends

I've come to realize that the most important thing is that I don't desensitize myself to lyrics. Sometimes, if I hear something over and over, I just sing it without thinking through the message. But it isn't just music and lyrics. It reflects me.

I recently accepted Christ into my life, and everything is going great! But I've been told that I shouldn't listen to secular music, and I was wondering why not. Why is secular music bad? Please help me. I'm going insane because I love music!

Chapter 4

My iPod Is Going Straight to My Thighs

 Pam: Music adds life and color to our world. Through the power of its emotional pull, it impacts us on a soul level, shaping our feelings.
Comment On This · Love This · Share with Friends

 Amanda: If I have an emotional reaction to music, I have to analyze it. I think we teenagers go clingy on songs that we can relate to or escape to or have fun with. So "Grenade" is just one of the many that I can get into when it comes to being "deep" about relationships. Ha! We all want our knight in shining armor. My dad died, so "The Soft Goodbye" gets to me in non-superficial times. A reaction is when a song makes me want to do SOMETHING other than just sit like a lump. For me, that would usually be making me want to draw or paint, because those are a big part of my life.
Comment On This · Love This · Share with Friends

 Garrett: I think people over-analyze the impact of music. It's entertainment that I have on to be on. I'm not going to go ballistic just because I have hip hop on, and I'm not going to start crying just because something soft is on. It is what it is.
Comment On This · Love This · Share with Friends

 Dan: Whatever! You can try and pretend its impact away. Maybe you aren't going to go ballistic. But the music will impact your mood. You can't deny that some beats make you happy, and others drag you down. That's a fact!
Comment On This · Love This · Share with Friends

 Emily: I'm 17 years old and a senior in high school. Being a Music Major, in the fall of 2011 anyway, I love music! I always have, and as a singer I love to find new songs that interest me—with both their melodies and their lyrics. Music influences people, especially teenagers—now more than ever!

I find that if I'm listening to Taylor Swift's songs about a boy or relationship, I apply it to my life and sometimes can become sad or depressed thinking about it. Not only that, but I also find myself thinking about a boy throughout the day! If I'm on my way to work, and I'm listening to a sad song about how a boy I like isn't falling in love with me, then I spend the next 3½ hours thinking about that, and it becomes exhausting! However, if I spend that time on my way to work listening to Hillsong or Jesus Culture, then I find my day is much more enjoyable because I spend my shift in the presence of God, and He shows me new and exciting things about Himself!

Don't get me wrong—Taylor Swift is an incredible artist! I love listening to her. I was just using some of her lyrics as an example. There are several other artists that have that effect: Justin Bieber, Selena Gomez, Rihanna or even Miley Cyrus and Demi Lovato. I still listen to those artists, but I choose a time when I'm hanging out with friends. I listen to Christian music a whole lot more, though, since I have recognized the effect secular music has had on my attitude.

Music is an expression; it can influence the way you treat other people and will help you choose how you are going to act throughout your day. It's so important not to let music take over your thinking. My dad always says, "Garbage in, garbage out." I want people to see God's love when they look at me. If all I'm thinking about is a boy or relationship, I can't show His everlasting, incredible love.

Comment On This · Love This · Share with Friends

📝 **Note: Music and the Human Soul.** Music is a unique form of media because it "hits" each of us differently depending on our mood, thoughts, beliefs and cultural values. Yet, it will ALWAYS reach deep within, touching the inner spirit. Music knows no barriers. As it is heard and interpreted, it colors the listener's perspective of the world, changing them. Though the reaction may look different for two different hearers, a response is sure to take place, and we are changed from the inside out.

 Coral: I really need help on this subject. I recently accepted Christ into my life, and everything is going great! But I've been told that I shouldn't listen to secular music, and I was wondering why not. Why is secular music bad? Please help me. I'm going insane because I love music!

Comment On This · Love This · Share with Friends

 Pam: Congratulations on your new life in Christ! What an amazing GIFT and blessing to know Christ's love and live with His guidance in your life.

It isn't that Christians can't listen to secular music. I certainly believe that there are many great songs sung by artists who are not a part of the Christian music genre. However, it is important to acknowledge that music is powerful. Everything you hear in your music—positive and negative—will influence you. This is why being cautious about the particular songs you choose to listen to is important.

Because you are a new Christian, my guess is that people are trying to enhance and strengthen your faith walk by suggesting that you listen to music that reinforces biblical messages rather than songs that may suck you back into the ways of the world. There are several "styles" of Christian music, so you can likely find someone whose songs will feed your faith through a similar sound to the secular artists whose music you enjoy.

That being said, DO NOT feel badly about appreciating ANY music as long as its message uplifts you, develops your character and brings you closer to Christ!

Comment On This • Love This • Share with Friends

Pam: "Music can change the world because it can change people" (Bono).
Comment On This • Love This • Share with Friends

Ally: So true. I woke up this morning still frustrated by a song stuck in my head. When I went to school, I couldn't focus. It seems ridiculous that a song could depress me to that degree!
Comment On This • Love This • Share with Friends

Lenny: If I'm honest with myself, I know that the way I see others is tainted by the music I listen to. Even if I have the best of intentions and say that I just like the beat or the group or whatever, the lyrics still run through my head over and over again. I can try to separate myself from it, but the messages sink in over time. It's an inescapable result.
Comment On This • Love This • Share with Friends

Todd: I always have conflicting feelings about music being blamed for some stuff—like when, a couple of years ago, there was a shooting in my home state of Ohio. A 14-year-old boy wearing a Marilyn Manson shirt shot four people in his high school before killing himself. A couple of days before the incident, reports say that he got in a fight with some other kids about who he worshipped, adamant that he didn't care about God and worshipped

Marilyn Manson.[1] Some people said the music was to blame or at least a contributor. But sometimes I feel like it is the scapegoat—a way to explain some messed-up kid's behavior just to answer the "why" question.

Comment On This · Love This · Share with Friends

Pam: The Ohio school shooting was not the first school shooting where music was linked to the shooter's actions. There have been SEVERAL devastating deathly events over the years whose perpetrators demonstrated an extreme love for heavy metal, rap and other frequently "angry" music.

I am not a violence expert, and whether or not the love for Marilyn Manson was actually enough to push this young man over the edge is not for me to say. I do not know his heart. However, I can confidently say that if he "worshipped" Marilyn Manson, then the lyrics to Manson's music would exert a powerful influence in his life. The dictionary defines "worship" as "the reverent love and devotion accorded a deity, an idol, or a sacred object." When used as a verb, "worship" means "to honor and love as a deity."

This young man claimed to worship Manson, so this means he honored Manson with his words, choices and life the way a Christian seeks to honor and love God! Is this Marilyn Manson's fault? Not directly. Marilyn Manson is free to make whatever music he wants, and he isn't the one who took violent action. But the power of what he heard in Manson's music was enough to, at minimum, affect this boy's apparel choice AND get him into a very vocal fight. The fact that music was a powerful influence in his life cannot be denied. He got defensive because of it, and he MAY have opened fire because of it. This should be enough to make everyone think about the weight of a person's musical listening choices. More importantly, it should cause us to consider WHOM WE WORSHIP!

Comment On This · Love This · Share with Friends

📰 **Newsflash:** The American Psychological Association confirms that violent music lyrics increase aggressive thoughts and feelings.[2]

Pam: Lord help us all! The pop icon Lady Gaga is now saying, "When you make music or write or create, it's really your job to have mind-blowing, irresponsible sex with whatever idea it is you're writing about at the time"?[3] What is she smoking?!

Comment On This · Love This · Share with Friends

Lily: I went to one of her concerts and she was giving away free condoms. It was kind of ridiculous.

Comment On This · Love This · Share with Friends

Emily: Well, after hearing all of her lyrics, some people probably wanted to use them . . . if you get my hint.

Comment On This · Love This · Share with Friends

Sarina: You changed my thoughts after I heard you speak. Too bad everyone doesn't know the truth about so-called safe sex and practice a little self-control!

Comment On This · Love This · Share with Friends

Becca: Well, in her song "Bad Romance" she says, "I want your disease." Good thing, 'cause if you use the condoms she passed out, you're going to get someone's disease!

Comment On This · Love This · Share with Friends

Denise: How about Rihanna singing in her song *S&M*, "Sticks and stones may break my bones but chains and whips excite me." If that isn't trying to create irresponsible, violent sex, I don't know what is!

Comment On This · Love This · Share with Friends

💕 Hailie's Story

Music has influenced me throughout my life. Depending on the age and stage of my life, the style and subject of the music has varied. As a young, elementary school-aged girl, I sang "The B-I-B-L-E" and found great comfort in "standing alone on the word of God."

However, in my middle school through college years, I changed. I still loved my church life and even loved God. Youth group was a huge part of my life, as were Bible study and prayer. At the same time that I was basically leading in my youth group, I was also taking part in various flirtatious friendships with guys my age as well as "falling in love" in a deep, heart-felt way with a few special guys throughout the course of those young years of my life. For me, those years were especially difficult because I was trying to figure out who I was and how to fit in with the various crowds around me. I thought I wanted to be different and not part of the crowd, but my actions proved otherwise. Even more important and heart-clenching for me was my interaction with those gorgeous, smooth-talking guys who made my knees weak just thinking of them.

In spite of everything I knew in my mind about the dangers of tiptoeing the line sexually as well as knowing how vital it is to "guard your heart, for it is the wellspring of life" (Proverbs 4:23), I could not resist the pull on my emotions and the boost to my self-esteem that came with the flirtatious, seemingly sincere smooth-talking of the boys I longed for. Sometimes it was just one special young man. Other times it was a couple at a time. They knew just what to say and how to say it. And, of course, they also knew just what to "do" and how to "do" it . . . even how to "do" it without crossing that imaginary, forbidden "line."

How did I recognize when these guys were saying and doing the "right" things? What shaped my idea of how I should be treated and spoken to by them?

No, not "The B-I-B-L-E" that I had grown up knowing, loving and standing on.

Music. And music videos.

One specific song comes to mind that even shaped my thinking in my late high school and early college years. I must admit, I still get a little googly-eyed and weak-kneed when I hear it in my head. I think my heart still skips a few beats. That's how much music affected me then; so much so that its effect lingers even now—in my mid-30s!

The song? "I'll Make Love to You" by Boyz II Men. The lyrics? Aren't they a bit obvious? They talk about making love, holding each other tight, throwing clothes on the floor, taking a long time, and promises to "give you the love of your life," in a very sensual combination of chords and smooth voices.

What girl would not feel extremely special and valued and loved if her "man" said those kinds of things to her? (And even more so if he sang those words to her the way Boyz II Men did!)

But seriously, words like those polluted my mind and began the slow scarring and callous-forming of my heart.

Words like those set up expectations in my mind for what my future husband should say to me and how he should act towards me. Because of those unrealistic and unfair expectations, I have had an extremely hard time accepting the kind of love my husband does give me. I have to fight off memories of past mistakes as well as let go of fairy-tale dreams I thought were supposed to be real and even expected of a husband-and-wife relationship.

I now choose deliberately to fill my mind with the TRUTH, including my music selection. I still occasionally enjoy secular songs, but overall I recognize what a battleground my mind is. I choose to fill my mind with truth, not Boyz II Men.

Newsflash: Teens who listen to music with sexually explicit, "dirty" or degrading messages are twice as likely to have intercourse or other sexual contact within two years than their peers who are exposed to little or no sexually degrading music.[4]

 Anastasia: Sexy lyrics do have a sexual effect on listeners. I start crying every time I hear "Amazed" by Lonestar. My ex-boyfriend and I considered that "our song." We first danced to it at the school dance when he asked me to "officially" be his girlfriend. We played it often when we were on our way home from a date—before things would "happen," if you know what I mean. He was the first guy I ever had sex with, and he broke up with me just a couple of days later. Every time I pass him in the hall, my heart aches over what I gave to him, and when I hear the song, I just bawl because I associate it so closely with him. I wish the song would just go away.

Comment On This · Love This · Share with Friends

 Pam: I am so sorry to hear of your heartache. Music has the potential to transport us to a specific event or time in our lives—sometimes positive, sometimes not.

Until you heal emotionally from the breakup, you will always hurt when you hear this song (and the association may never completely go away). So, it is important that you seek good Christian help. I would suggest calling 1-800-395-HELP to reach your local crisis pregnancy center. While most people assume such centers are only there for pregnancy tests, that is not true! They offer a variety of services, including relationship counseling. This would give you the opportunity to speak one-on-one with a trained counselor about your relationship, the decisions you made, forgiveness, breaking bonds, and establishing new boundaries that will help you make wiser dating choices in the future. Please give them a call today.

Anastasia, it is also possible that you could have become infected with an STD. If you have not gotten tested, please do so for the sake of yourself and your future spouse.

I would also strongly suggest that you do some reading to accompany your counseling. In the first book in this series, *Nobody Told Me,* we offer advice that will help you see that you are not alone and be empowered for a healthy future.[5]

Comment On This · Love This · Share with Friends

 Lindsey: Your message is definitely inspiring. I have watched several of your videos, and they're awesome. I think it's so important to tell teens about the consequences of sex, and how important the decision to have sex is. One of my least favorite songs is "Break Your Heart" by Taio Cruz. It's a very catchy song, but the message is terrible. The guy is a player, and he tells the girl he's only going to break her heart. It's an upbeat, popular song about getting used and dumped. Whenever I hear this on the radio, I think about how glamorized pre-marital sex is, and how much damage it can cause in people's lives. This type of music is completely destructive, but it has hit the mainstream and gets glamorized beyond belief. PLEASE keep up your good work!

Comment On This · Love This · Share with Friends

Leo: Can I just say as a guy that I hate this song—and many others like it! Why are guys always portrayed as these aggressors who get their "manhood" from using women? It's not the image I want to have!

Comment On This · Love This · Share with Friends

 Trista: Not the image you want to have?! I'm so glad Lindsey posted this, because I'm sick of music telling girls that it is okay to be used and abused by guys who couldn't care less about them. These songs make it seem as though we were made to sexually gratify men. There is so much more to the people God created us to be, and yet from the time we are little and have the radio on, all we hear are these sickening songs about being lust objects for horny guys. Too many girls fall into the trap of believing that is true.

Comment On This · Love This · Share with Friends

 Pam: We must remember that NEITHER gender is properly represented here. I meet guys around the world all the time who have integrity and are saving themselves for their future wives. They have confidence in their "manhood" because they are treating women with respect. I also meet girls who proudly display purity rings and set boundaries, knowing their bodies were designed for their husbands alone.

Oppositely, I meet members of both genders who have fallen into the stereotype these lyrics promote. These are the guys who ask me how they are going to get a "good wife" after what they've done, and girls who are crying because they really believed that if they had sex, it would somehow equal love, and the relationship would last forever.

The critical point here is, don't take relationship lessons from music. Take advice from the expert on relationships and love— God—through His Word! Please take a moment to carefully read 1 Corinthians 13! Do the messages in the music you are listening to reflect what God says love is?

Comment On This · Love This · Share with Friends

 Pam: I was just out at the mall and noticed girls-sized shirts that said, "Future Mrs. Bieber"! We're idolizing everyday, fallible people who have become "stars," and we're teaching young people that it's okay to do that. This is a dangerous road!

Comment On This · Love This · Share with Friends

MacKenzie: I hope I'm the future Mrs. Bieber!
Comment On This · Love This · Share with Friends

 Amy: No, me! He's doing a concert in my area, and my parents won't let me see my future husband because they say his tickets cost too much. Lame!
Comment On This · Love This · Share with Friends

 Joel: You girls' infatuation is what is lame! Hello, he doesn't even know who you are!
Comment On This · Love This · Share with Friends

 Leah: It just goes to show how influential celebrities are in our society. We wear dorky clothing with their pictures on it, dress like them and call it a "trend," and watch their every move. When you think about it, it's crazy.
Comment On This · Love This · Share with Friends

@ **Link:** Speaking of crazy, check out this insane video. A three-year-old is CRYING over Justin Bieber! http://www.youtube.com/watch?v=dTCm8tdHkfI&feature=share

 MyKayla: Most certainly insane!
Comment On This · Love This · Share with Friends

 Caitlin: Actually, I think I feel like that sometimes. Embarrassing!
Comment On This · Love This · Share with Friends

 Sam: That is ridiculous!
Comment On This · Love This · Share with Friends

✎ **Note: Idol Worship. It Isn't Just Statues!** "You shall have no other gods before Me. You shall not make for yourself a carved image—any likeness of anything that is in heaven above, or that is in the earth beneath, or that is in the water under the earth; you shall not bow down to them or serve them. For I, the LORD your God, am a jealous God" (Exodus 20:3-5, *NKJV*). The First and Second Commandments are really about loyalty. The creator of the universe declares that He is our God. As our deliverer, He asks us to demonstrate our love for Him by having no other gods.

Establishing, developing and maintaining a personal relationship with the true and living God is the most important commitment we can ever make and should be our number one priority. In fact, it is the primary focus in the FIRST of the Ten Commandments: "You shall have no other gods before Me." We should love, honor and respect God so much that He alone is the supreme authority and model in our lives because He alone is God. NEVER should we allow anything or anyone to prevent us from serving and obeying Him.

With these ideas in mind, think about the way many rock stars are treated by their fans. I am seeing screaming girls, practically fainting, running for the stage. I will never forget the young girl who cried hysterically while listening to Sanjaya sing (really? of all people?) and became an instant YouTube phenomenon. Do a quick Google search on *American Idol crying fans* and you will see literally hundreds of examples of this madness.

Would it surprise anyone that many of these "fans" can quote every lyric to every song by their favorite musicians, as well as tell you almost everything about them, including their favorite colors or fast food chains? Probably not. But could these same teens quote even ONE verse of Scripture or tell you any detail about the life of Christ—besides that He was born in a stable on Christmas?

Is "worshipping" these stars really wrong? Does it really matter if you have a "teen idol" or "crush"? Will it really affect your life? Well, what would it look like if we had a "crush" on Jesus? What if we spent as much time seeking to KNOW everything about Jesus as we spend learning countess details about Lady Gaga or Katy Perry? What if we actually CARED as much about what Jesus has to say about our choices in clothes, music, friends and hobbies as we value the opinions of Rihanna or Usher? What if we seriously asked ourselves "What Would Jesus Do" instead of "What Would Justin Bieber, or Lil Wayne, Do?" I challenge you to try. It might actually change your life!

 Marin: Remember the freak-out over David Archuleta losing?
Comment On This · Love This · Share with Friends

 Anya: How about Taylor Swift? She is kind of like the female version of Justin Bieber. People are OBSESSED.
Comment On This · Love This · Share with Friends

 Laura: What an interesting challenge! While I love the Lord, I would NEVER have compared the time I spend thinking about a star's life to how much I seek to know about Christ's. Thank you for making me think!
Comment On This · Love This · Share with Friends

 Brittany: Great note, Pam! I babysit this little girl who asks me to sing her "love-a-bies." Her favorite is "How Great Is Our God." She knows whom to idolize!
Comment On This · Love This · Share with Friends

 Pam: Adorable!
Comment On This · Love This · Share with Friends

Jenny: You mentioned Lady Gaga in your post. Did you see her on *Good Morning America* in her condom dress? I hope people don't try to mimic that look!

Comment On This · Love This · Share with Friends

 Pam: Interestingly, Gaga wore that hideous condom dress for Acquired Immune Deficiency Syndrome (AIDS) Awareness week to promote "safe" sex. Apparently no one told Gaga that latex condoms have holes in them called voids. According to Dr. C. Michael Roland, editor of *Rubber Chemistry and Technology*, the Human Immunodeficiency Virus (which causes AIDS) is 50 times smaller than these voids, taking the "safe" out of "safe sex"![6] How tragic that fans looking up to her will see and believe the wrong message. There is a way to prevent AIDS and all other (more common) STDs. It's called ABSTINENCE and being FAITHFUL in marriage!

Comment On This · Love This · Share with Friends

Newsflash: Researchers at the University of Texas analyzed 11 studies regarding the condom's effectiveness in preventing AIDS transmission. They concluded that the average condom failure rate in preventing AIDS was an astonishing 31%.[7]

 Pam: "Music washes away from the soul the dust of everyday life" (Berthold Auerbach).

Comment On This · Love This · Share with Friends

 Kelly: What a beautiful image!

Comment On This · Love This · Share with Friends

 Rebecca: I experience this feeling when I listen to "In Christ Alone." There is so much substance and feeling to that song.

Comment On This · Love This · Share with Friends

 Lori: "Here I Am to Worship" by Hillsong helps me. It's such a wonderful reminder of God's love for me and the importance of bowing down in order to experience His best!

Comment On This · Love This · Share with Friends

 Courtney: Christian music brings me peace too, but there are some great musicians in other genres that provide the same feeling. Carrie Underwood's "Jesus Take the Wheel" is one of the best songs out there. The idea of relinquishing control to Christ takes so much pressure off of me!

Comment On This · Love This · Share with Friends

Barbie: When I was pregnant, I used to sing Elton John's "You'll Be Blessed" to my child in utero. Regardless of how the day went, there was so much peace in singing that song and dreaming of our baby. It had such a positive pro-life message!

Comment On This · Love This · Share with Friends

💚 Melissa's Story

I'll never forget that moment in the hospital room. Early that morning, my father's doctor had called to let us know that it was only going to be a few hours before my father would be trading Earth for the streets paved with gold. I put on his windbreaker that I always made fun of for being so bright, made some phone calls and went to his ICU room. After the nurse assured me that he could still hear, I took his hand and bared my heart. I told my dad all that I was thankful for and all that I would do.

Moments later, the monitor flat-lined. Even though I knew this moment was coming, and I'd tried to prepare myself for it as much as I could, when it finally arrived, I panicked. I wanted someone to grab the paddles and shock my dad back to life like on *ER*. But life isn't a television show. Jesus' ways aren't always depicted on TV.

I was only in college. When I returned to school I did my best to balance healthy sharing with not raking myself over the emotional coals. In my typical Type A, perfectionist way, I tried to somehow compartmentalize time for dealing with my feelings, so that I could still be successful in the classroom.

However, when the day was done, and the "stuff" of the world was no longer keeping me busy, I would sit and think, which led to sadness and tears. The grief was overwhelming, and oftentimes I didn't know how to pray. I was speechless, teetering on the edge between two ideas of how to cope—healthily in Christ or in the failing ways of my own strength.

Music has always been a meaningful part of my life. I sang at church, and I listened to music while studying and at various other times. Music intensifies joy on life's mountaintops and acknowledges pain in the midst of hardship. I don't let a day pass without listening to music.

During that difficult period in my life, Rich Mullins's "Hold Me Jesus" spoke words that I could not. Truth be told, it became the words to my prayer. Proverbs 3:5-6 says, "Trust in the LORD with all your heart and lean not on your own understanding; in all your ways submit to him, and he will make your paths straight." When I turned on Rich Mullins's song, tears would flow in a healthy way. I could bare my unmasked soul to God, and in the midst of my brokenness, He began to piece back together hope and confidence, helping me to move forward in life with faith.

Acknowledging who He is, and who I was not, in the midst of such intense pain helped me yield to His ways and pulled me into His loving, safe embrace. I listened to that song over and over each day to keep my focus where it should be and assure genuine healing. As the words articulated, my life didn't make sense. Life's mountains did look big, and I was shaking like a leaf. Even though darkness hurt, surrender didn't come naturally to me. (Remember, I'm a perfectionist. I like control!) Eventually, as the lyrics beautifully say, I'd fall on my knees, resistance thinning, and I'd allow the King of Glory to be my Prince of Peace. The song met me where I was and led me to where I needed to be.

Praise God for musical messages that give voice to our experience and bind us to our Father, Healer and Redeemer. This is music used for good!

 Jesse: I think music has always been one of the most important "medicines" when you are hurting deeply. Recently, when I went through a huge loss, I picked up Steven Curtis Chapman's *Beauty Will Rise*. He wrote the songs on this album after losing his little adopted daughter in a horrible accident, and they take you through his journey of despair, faith and hope. Listening to those lyrics really helped me get out all the emotions I was experiencing in my own grief!

Comment On This • Love This • Share with Friends

 Pam: Thanks for sharing your personal journey of grief and healing. The album is a great suggestion!

Comment On This • Love This • Share with Friends

📰 **Newsflash:** "Christian music is the fastest-growing area of radio."[8]

 Billy: I have always loved music because it draws me closer to the Lord. Unlike my television, Xbox and computer that I use for entertainment, music is IN Scripture. When the king needed calming, David would play his lyre and "relief would come to Saul; he would feel better, and the evil spirit would leave him" (1 Samuel 16:23). Music has brought peace to people throughout the ages, and hearing words that come from Scripture or reinforce biblical messages is an entertaining way to get to know God better. I love it!

Comment On This • Love This • Share with Friends

 Pam: How true! Unlike most of modern media, music is referred to in the Bible time and time again. Having the opportunity to hear a song that is a balm to the spirit or lyrics that come from the Bible strengthens our belief as those messages take root in our hearts. This leads to outward joy and the spreading of faith. I'm reminded of Psalm 138:5: "May they sing of the ways of the LORD, for the glory of the LORD is great"!

Comment On This • Love This • Share with Friends

Krista: I've come to realize that the most important thing is that I don't desensitize myself to lyrics and what I'm singing about. Sometimes, if I hear something over and over, I just sing it without thinking through the message it is sending. But it isn't just music and lyrics. It reflects me.

Comment On This · Love This · Share with Friends

 Pam: Yes! The key for all of us is to remember that it isn't so much whether we are listening to Christian or secular musicians, but that we MUST be mindful of the messages sent in the songs we are listening to. Our words, whether spoken or "sung," reflect our character and at the deepest soul level impact our moral fiber.

Comment On This · Love This · Share with Friends

 Pam: The same power that music has for good, the enemy can use to destroy our souls. What are you listening to?

Comment On This · Love This · Share with Friends

Chapter 5

I've Been Gaming So Long I Have a Mountain Dew High

 Pam: Fantasy turns to reality as each video gaming platform seeks to make your experience of the game bigger and better.
Comment On This · Love This · Share with Friends

 Paul: I'm totally guilty of blowing my entire paycheck on a new game today!
Comment On This · Love This · Share with Friends

 Althea: Video games are awesome because you can socialize with a bunch of people through the multi-player games like *World of Warcraft*. Gaming rocks! You escape life and make new friends.
Comment On This · Love This · Share with Friends

 Tony: No kidding! The multi-player role-playing games are like having a party with friends without having them all in your house. Makes the parents and me happy. Win-Win!
Comment On This · Love This · Share with Friends

 Zara: I love Wii tennis. It's so cool that technology has come so far that the direction my wrist is facing actually impacts the way my ball goes. Having friends over and playing doubles is the best!
Comment On This · Love This · Share with Friends

Newsflash: 80% of teens between 12 and 17 own a gaming console of some kind. More males than females own them, with 89% of boys having a gaming system compared to 70% of girls.[1]

 Kari: I have definite opinions on this. My husband has played video games since he was little. There have been times in the distant past when he has played every single day for WEEKS, at which points I have accused him of "being addicted." He always says he is not. Over time, he has proven to me that his gaming is not an addiction, but a hobby. However, I don't think video games are a healthy hobby. I think they take people away from human interaction.
Comment On This · Love This · Share with Friends

Pam: The two words that you have chosen to use in your post—addiction and hobby—are exactly what I want all teenagers to think through. Clearly games in and of themselves are not bad things. However, moderation and content are important in maintaining a healthy, normal balance between LIFE and PLAY.

As children are exposed to these games at younger and younger ages, you are correct that habits can be formed early on. Such habits may follow these youthful gamers throughout their lives (as you have seen). Temperament is important when considering time spent playing video games. Individuals who tend to struggle with social relationships—who are withdrawn or "loners" by nature—are more likely to shut themselves off from the real world and escape into the gaming world because it fits their comfort levels. Obviously, for these people, recognizing that "pulling back" like this is leading to decreased social skills—and then turning off the gaming system—is important. Those who have a little bit more of an outgoing personality—who are interested in sports and extracurricular activities, and achieve success in school—are more likely to have a balanced approach to gaming, at which point it can actually be a fun hobby.

Content is also important to consider. What individuals see and actively participate in while playing these games WILL shape their worldviews. So, if hours are spent with a game that promotes violence, sex, building fake worlds where players exercise complete control, or engaging in extreme competition, it can be hard to transition back into the "real world," where we are called to practice self-control, work with others and submit to God's will.

I'm thankful to hear of the discussions that have happened in your home. The key is for gamers to recognize how their play affects their everyday lives, so they don't make decisions they will later regret or destroy the relationships that are most important to them.

Comment On This · Love This · Share with Friends

Gina: I found your comment in the last wall post about submitting to God's will and control issues in games to be interesting. I am a major *Sims* fan. But my friends and I sometimes joke about other people in our classes, saying their lives are "the *Sims* game I would totally delete." That is the thing about *Sims*. You get to live in this virtual world where you get to control everything, and if it isn't exactly what you want, you can delete it and start over. There is satisfaction in that, because you always get the life you want. But when you turn the game off and enter reality, it isn't like that. I don't get control—and that's frustrating.

Comment On This · Love This · Share with Friends

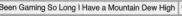
 Pam: Isaiah 55:8 comes to mind: "'For my thoughts are not your thoughts, neither are your ways my ways,' declares the LORD." Wanting control is a natural human tendency, and these games can certainly exacerbate that desire, causing increased frustration with everyday life.

The interesting thing about these games is that they assume (or make us believe) we know what is best for a fulfilling, successful life. However, in reality, we have a very limited worldview. Unlike God, who can see past, present AND future, we can only see the past and have very limited understanding, at best, of the present. How then can we really know what is best, let alone determine what person's life warrants the "delete" button?

For you to be happy, you will need to admit that the game is only a game and be THANKFUL for that fact. When you let go of believing that you know what is best for life and yield to God's control, you will experience true satisfaction. He can see the big picture. We can't.

Comment On This · Love This · Share with Friends

 Pam: "You do anything long enough to escape the habit of living until the escape becomes the habit" (David Ryan). Are your games a fun escape or an addictive habit?

Comment On This · Love This · Share with Friends

 Brady: I got *Saints Row 2* from a friend. It's sort of a violent game, but I wanted to play it all the time. My mom restricted the time that I could play, and I'm actually thankful that she did. My grades started getting better, and that helped me to feel better about myself. Now I can control it on my own.

Comment On This · Love This · Share with Friends

 Joanna: I play *Sims*! It gets really addicting sometimes, and mainly I've learned to control it by taking out the disk and leaving it in another room. Sometimes I'll have my mom hide it (seems silly but it works!). The bad thing about *Sims* is that you can't only play it for a half-hour.

Comment On This · Love This · Share with Friends

 Julie: I was so hooked on *Sims*! (Obviously before life with children.) Even at my age (not a teen!), I wished I had more time to play—any time to play! Like Joanna says, you can't play *Sims* for just half an hour. You need a decent chunk of time to . . . commit.

Comment On This · Love This · Share with Friends

Austin: Sports titles are fun and competitive. I like that you can pick them up, play them and then let them go. They aren't ongoing, so they don't weigh on your mind.

Comment On This · Love This · Share with Friends

 Lacey: Our family has game night, and we sometimes play Wii games. Definitely a fun escape!

Comment On This · Love This · Share with Friends

 Armida: I don't play, but I can tell you about my 13-year-old brother. He is certainly addicted to video games—you know, the violent ones. He goes crazy if my mom doesn't let him play, and once he starts playing, he won't stop until someone pries the controller out of his hands. He plays for about three hours at a time.

Comment On This · Love This · Share with Friends

@ **Link:** Some of you (boys!) had a good laugh at all the girls freaking out over Justin Bieber in the last chapter. So, to make things fair, I think we all need to take a look at the BOYS freaking out over *World of Warcraft*! This really amazed me! http://www.youtube.com/watch?v=YerslyzsOpc

🐱 Nathan's Story

 My life as a gamer started when I was probably four years old. My first game console was Super Nintendo. I played many different varieties of games. Soon I was beating games pretty fast, so I started renting them instead of buying them. I always looked forward to a new game or challenge. Once I discovered online play, I was hooked. Playing *Socom* and *Star Wars Galaxies* online offered new adventures and thrills. I played large numbers of hours, trying to compete with other gamers.

These last five years, I've been playing *World of Warcraft*. I became so concentrated on gaming that I lost focus on goals in life. Spending massive hours on gaming instead of my studies, I soon dropped out of college, and many other problems followed. I couldn't hold down a decent job, and I watched my life spiral downhill from there.

I know that I am not alone in this addictive world. I was playing instead of living real life. Many people I know have gone down the same road—giving a lot of time to playing online games, and having many challenges in life because of this addiction. I understand these online games can be a fun way to escape life, but I also know the serious problems they can cause. These games can have unexpected consequences for newer gamers if they are not aware of the risks.

Too much of anything is bad for you, but knowing when to quit is the hardest thing. Spending or wasting time on these games can affect your life greatly, and there are no warning signs like on a pack of cigarettes. Maybe the games should have warning labels like cigarettes do.

The main thing people need to know is that when gaming starts taking over their daily living, it is too much, and they need to find a balance between real life and the game. Quitting completely is hard, I know. I still play off and on. I enjoy online gaming because it passes the time and it's socially satisfying.

However, I've learned that talking to a computer screen for eight hours straight is not the same as talking directly to another human being. We have to learn to draw the line when we notice red flags telling us we are out of control. In game and out, we must be aware of what we are dealing with, and we must pay attention to our behaviors.

I have nothing against gaming. As I said, to this day I love and enjoy playing—in moderation, and in harmony with the rest of my life. Once you figure out a good balance, stick with it and have fun. I hope my story can reach out and make people aware of some circumstances this addiction can bring. I wish my fellow gamers the best. Happy gaming!

David: I enjoy player vs. computer games immensely, but I find them too addictive, so I have had to give them up completely. If I didn't, they could consume all my time. I physically broke a disc of my favorite computer game to break the addiction. Later I bought another one and had to break that one too.

Comment On This · Love This · Share with Friends

Pam: GOOD FOR YOU, David, for recognizing your addiction and taking steps to break it. If gaming is an addictive behavior for you, separating yourself from it NOW is imperative so it doesn't ruin your life later. Continue to STAND STRONG!

Comment On This · Love This · Share with Friends

Newsflash: Approximately 1 in 10 gaming youth is scientifically classified as addicted. Among the consequences of gaming addiction are "depression, anxiety, social phobias and lower school performance."[2]

Pam: As an abstinence speaker, I am horrified by the "normalized" sex scenes in some of these games. Where has God's boundary for sex gone?

Comment On This · Love This · Share with Friends

Kathleen: Games like *God of War* have sex mini-games, within the game itself, where if you have the main character have sex with these Greek women, you get life or game points. I do think that affects character.

Comment On This · Love This · Share with Friends

Todd: You would really hate *Grand Theft Auto*. You can visit prostitutes to REGAIN your health. Like it is good for you. The whole point of the game is sex and mass murder.

Comment On This · Love This · Share with Friends

Danielle: That doesn't even sound like the worst of it. My boyfriend was telling me about some scene in a newer version that seems to encourage cheating on girlfriends and actually shows some girl, who is wearing barely anything, performing oral sex. I was so offended I told him to stop, but for some reason he went on to tell me that you can change your viewing angle, and that to win you have to get the "excitement meter" to the top. GROSS! I was so mad we got into a big fight. As his girlfriend, I feel disrespected that he is okay looking at this trash, and I told him we were through if he ever plays it again.

Comment On This · Love This · Share with Friends

Devon: Don't be dissin' this game. I know it doesn't treat relationships with women well, but it is one of the best games ever! I love it!

Comment On This · Love This · Share with Friends

Blake: As a 17-year-old boy, I want the girls reading this to know that not all of us boys think this is cool. It makes me really mad that picking up prostitutes and simulating sex is supposed to be fun. It makes me even madder that "all guys" have an image for liking it. So, girls, know that there are a lot of us boys who know this goes against the Bible, and we have enough respect for you to stay away from it.

Comment On This · Love This · Share with Friends

Siri: I want to find a guy like you, Blake!

Comment On This · Love This · Share with Friends

Max: I have to be honest: I didn't think much about sex in video games until I was playing a game with some guys in my dorm room, and they were laughing about what they were doing to and with the girls. A light bulb turned on, and I thought, *We are not completely separate from this.* I haven't played a dirty game since.

Comment On This · Love This · Share with Friends

Pam: From my perspective, too many female characters in games boil down to "cartoon porn." Their attire is basically nothing, not to mention the exaggerated physique painted as "normal" in the minds of boys playing the games. You cannot tell me that looking at and acting out with these girls will not translate into a tainted view and utter disrespect for women, their bodies and their mental abilities. The creators of these games have reduced women to over-exaggerated body parts. As a woman, I find that insulting.

You saw the game perspective translate to the everyday life perspective when you witnessed these other boys laughing at and enjoying what they were virtually doing with these girls. Your story is a sad testament to what is happening in dorm rooms and homes around the country, and society will suffer as a result of this mind-set. Thank you for choosing character and eliminating these games from your life.

Comment On This · Love This · Share with Friends

 Pam: "I will not look with approval on anything that is vile. I hate what faithless people do; I will have no part in it. The perverse of heart shall be far from me; I will have nothing to do with what is evil" (Psalm 101:3-4). Is this true of your video games?

Comment On This · Love This · Share with Friends

 Tre: For this to be true, people would have to avoid all first-person shooter games that have sex and graphic violence. That doesn't leave a lot.

Comment On This · Love This · Share with Friends

 Pam: Is it more important to have a lot of choices or to fill your mind with the healthy choices that are out there?

Comment On This · Love This · Share with Friends

 Ryan: The first-person shooter games deaden one's mind to killing anyway. Why waste time with them?

Comment On This · Love This · Share with Friends

 Tre: I think people make more out of the idea of game violence leading to real-life violence than they should. It's an inflated claim.

Comment On This · Love This · Share with Friends

 Jonathan: I've recently become addicted to my Xbox 360, and I have noticed changes in myself with it. My grades have dropped, and my attitude is more vicious than it used to be. I've got to chill before I actually snap at someone.

Comment On This · Love This · Share with Friends

☞ **Note:** *Grand Theft Auto* **and a Brutal Murder.** Since some think the gaming violence /life violence link is overstated, I thought you should see this excerpt from a news story!

> *Grand Theft Auto* is a world governed by the laws of depravity. See a car you like? Steal it. Someone you don't like? Stomp her. A cop in your way? Blow him away.
>
> There are police at every turn, and endless opportunities to take them down. It is 360 degrees of murder and mayhem: slickly produced, technologically brilliant, and exceedingly violent.
>
> And now, the game is at the center of a civil lawsuit involving the murders of three men in the small town of Fayette, Alabama. They were gunned down by 18-year-old Devin Moore, who had played *Grand Theft Auto* day and night for months.
>
> Attorney Jack Thompson, a long-time crusader against video-game violence, is bringing the suit. "What we're saying is that Devin Moore was, in effect, trained to do what he did. He was given a murder simulator," says Thompson.
>
> "He bought it as a minor. He played it hundreds of hours, which is primarily a cop-killing game. It's our theory, which we think we can prove to a jury in Alabama, that, but for the video-game training, he would not have done what he did."
>
> Moore's victims were Ace Mealer, a 911 dispatcher; James Crump, a police officer; and Arnold Strickland, another officer who was on patrol in the early morning hours of June 7, 2003, when he brought in Moore on suspicion of stealing a car.
>
> Moore had no criminal history, and was cooperative as Strickland booked him inside the Fayette police station. Then suddenly, inexplicably, Moore snapped.
>
> According to Moore's own statement, he lunged at Officer Arnold Strickland, grabbing his .40-caliber Glock semi-automatic and shot Strickland twice, once in the head. Officer James Crump heard the shots and came running. Moore met him in the hallway, and fired three shots into Crump, one of them in the head.
>
> Moore kept walking down the hallway towards the door of the emergency dispatcher. There, he turned and fired five shots into Ace Mealer. Again, one of those shots was in the head. Along the way, Moore had grabbed a set of car keys. He went out the door to the parking lot, jumped into a police cruiser, and took off. It all took less than a minute, and three men were dead.
>
> "The video game industry gave him a cranial menu that popped up in the blink of an eye, in that police station," says Thompson. "And that menu offered him the split-second decision to kill the officers, shoot them in the head, flee in a police car, just as the game itself trained them to do."
>
> After his capture, Moore is reported to have told police, "Life is like a video game. Everybody's got to die sometime."[3]

Tre: Okay. Maybe this was an isolated incident.
Comment On This · Love This · Share with Friends

 Sara: Or maybe it is just time to admit that the link might actually be real.
Comment On This · Love This · Share with Friends

 Tracy: How sad!
Comment On This · Love This · Share with Friends

Newsflash: "More than 70 percent of American teenage boys have played the violent but popular 'Grand Theft Auto' video games, and they are more likely to have been in a fight than those who have not played."[4]

 Vance: Do you think we just don't care about the violence in video games because we've become desensitized to it?
Comment On This · Love This · Share with Friends

Pam: That's a good question, and one that I have spent a lot of time thinking about. Recently I picked up a *Rolling Stone* magazine in the airport as I was doing research for this book (I would normally NEVER read this magazine!). As I paged through the articles during my flight, I came across one that was so disturbing I literally almost got sick on the plane. The article was "The Kill Team,"[5] and it chronicled the demented plot by Bravo Company's 3rd platoon (part of the 5th Stryker Brigade out of Tacoma, Washington) to kill innocent civilians in Afghanistan. Not only was I unable to stomach reading the entire article, but I also could not BEAR to look at the photos, which were absolutely horrifying.

The article began by describing the murder of an unarmed 15-year-old Afghan boy who was brutally killed with a grenade while simultaneously being shot with an M4 carbine and a machine gun. I will not go into further detail. It was absolutely sickening. What caused this group of soldiers to behave this way? What had so seared their consciences that they could think this kind of carnage was acceptable—so much so that they would permanently "mark" their conquests with tattoos?

The psychological community will be debating this for decades, but I could not help wondering if the proliferation of violent video games has produced a culture where killing is mundane—where taking out "enemies" gets you points and praise, and where if you get shot or hurt in the process, one of your buddies just "heals" you and gives you more life to continue the destruction?

I don't know. What I do know is that research suggests that violent video games are creating violent people, and that seeing the actions in the games gives players "ideas" for real life. This makes me sad. All life is sacred. It isn't to be disregarded in such horrific ways. Until our culture is willing to say, "I won't buy this game or music or support these movies or TV," junk will continue to be produced. It is time to take a stand!

Comment On This · Love This · Share with Friends

Newsflash: A study published in the *Psychological Bulletin* reported a definitive link between violent video games and "increased aggressive thoughts and behavior, and decreased empathy" in youth.[6]

Note: Insight into Media Violence from an Expert. Colonel David Grossman is an expert and author on media violence.[7] I love his perspective here and had to share with everyone! Enjoy!

We have to think of violence like we would think of heart disease. It really is a soul-disease, if you will. And many things cause heart disease. There's obesity, overweight, does that cause heart disease? Yes. Does a high cholesterol diet, or stress, or lack of exercise, or genetics—do all those things cause heart disease? Yes, we know they do. If you take all the existing factors, and add tobacco to it, the result is an explosion of heart disease, anywhere in the world.

Well, in the same way, I want you to ask yourself what causes violent crime, or causes people to kill. Well, poverty, gangs, drugs, availability of guns, child abuse, family breakdown—these are all important factors. But what we *know* is that if you take the existing factors, and add the media violence—television, movie, and especially now the video-game violence—the result is an *explosion* of violent crime in any nation in which it takes place. . . .

These video games are simulators. There are flight simulators, that teach you how to fly. And there are murder simulators, whose only redeeming social value is that they teach you how to commit the act of murder. If these things were rape simulators, we would not tolerate letting our children play them. And yet we sit and watch our children play endless hours, practicing blowing people's heads off.

Now, my friends, people are going to say this. They're going to say, well, you know, that's just kids playing games. We played caps when we were kids; you all remember playing caps? We had toy guns. And I said, "Bang, bang, I got you, Billy." And Billy said, "No, you didn't." So, I smacked him with my cap gun. And he cried, and he went to his Momma, and I got in *big* trouble. And you know what I learned? I learned that Billy's real. And when I hurt Billy, bad things are going to happen to me.

Now, in the violent video games, I blow Billy's stinkin' head off in explosions of blood, countless thousands of times. And do I get trouble? No. I get points.[8]

Don: I am a police officer, and Colonel Grossman's lecture called "The Bullet Proof Mind" helped me tremendously after the shooting I was involved in.

Comment On This · Love This · Share with Friends

Ann: I love the comparison to soul disease. What a beautiful image.

Comment On This · Love This · Share with Friends

Jacob: Even as a boy, I was struck by this "soul disease" concept. With *Call of Duty*, and other games like that, you can play online against other real people, and that is what makes the games so great. But when you "die" you feel real embarrassment and, sadly, you feel good making other people "die" and feel embarrassed. This is not the person that I want to be.

Comment On This · Love This · Share with Friends

Katie: I saw your post and just wanted to encourage you that you are not alone. When you win in the game, you get a sense of accomplishment, so I've found myself wanting to play more to get that feeling more—but that means inviting more violence into my life. It's odd to acknowledge that I desire that.

Comment On This · Love This · Share with Friends

Pam: I've read that game playing triggers the release of dopamine in the brain.[9] When this neurotransmitter is released, there is a "feel-good" response that accompanies the pleasure, reward and exploration involved in these games. This same chemical is released when a smoker takes a puff on a cigarette or an addict snorts cocaine. The result is addiction, and it's powerful.

Because of this connection, even if you are concerned about how the game is impacting you on a personal level, it will continue to do so because of the powerful chemical force behind it. To break yourself from that "soul-level" sickness, you will have to STOP playing the games that are producing these overwhelming responses.

Comment On This · Love This · Share with Friends

📝 **Note: To Play or Not to Play.** Oftentimes people ask if they should be playing a video game or not. There are several GREAT games that my family enjoys playing together, so we have had to figure out the important questions to ask ourselves about games to determine if they are worthy of playing. This is a helpful "barometer" by youth minister Scott Firestone IV.[10]

I've been playing video games for over 30 years, so I've seen how they've changed over time. We've moved from comically jumping on heads to blowing them off. And the level of immersion has reached new heights of realism. But we have to ask ourselves if we're immersing ourselves in an unhealthy world.

Video games can teach us some great things. They teach tenacity, and that failure isn't the end. They can help us think creatively about how to solve a problem. And they can help us concentrate—the only time my six-year-old holds still for more than 30 seconds is when he's reading a Star Wars book and when he's playing video games. But there are some not-so-great things about video games, too.

I'll never forget when I reviewed the first *God of War* game. There was extreme violence and nudity—and that was bad—but there's a point in the game where you have to sacrifice an innocent man in order to progress. He's in a cage; you pull a lever; he burns up. There's no alternate route—no way to get around that single, horrible act. The producers of the game would probably argue that the guy wasn't real—that he's just pixels on a screen. That's true . . . but why did I feel so dirty afterward? That was a watershed moment where I realized the video game industry would do *anything* in the name of "entertainment."

I've never played a Massively Multiplayer Online (MMO) game—*World of Warcraft, Everquest* and so forth. I remember my father telling me about a co-worker of his who lived and breathed *Everquest.* He stayed up late playing, he would talk to people on the phone about it during work, and he let it overtake his life—and that was 10 years ago when the technology was new! This story removed any interest I had in playing those games. Games can be just as addictive as any other behavior. So ask yourself, *Has playing video games decreased my social interaction with real people? Have I blown off class or tests or schoolwork to play games? Are the games forcing me to make decisions that are immoral? If I do have a choice in the game, do I find myself making the immoral choice?* If so, it might be time to cut back—or better yet, quit cold turkey. Take some time off and create some rules and boundaries for yourself. And then stick to them! "Finally, brothers and sisters, whatever is true, whatever is noble, whatever is right, whatever is pure, whatever is lovely, whatever is admirable—if anything is excellent or praiseworthy—think about such things" (Philippians 4:8).

I'm not anti-video games—I still play them all the time! But I do have to constantly ask myself if they're interfering with my walk with God, or with my relationship with my family. And then I have to be strong enough to make the hard choice if the answer to those questions is yes.

 Judy: When it comes down to it, I think we entertain ourselves way too much, and that turns the mind into mush. We need to use our minds—to think, to be creative, to affect the lives of others for good, and to bring about change in the world. Being creative is part of God's imaginative stamp upon our lives, and not to utilize that God-given ability is to dishonor Him. Games that promote healthy relationships and exercise the mind have my vote.

Comment On This · Love This · Share with Friends

 Pam: WELL stated, Judy! Games can be wonderful GIFTS if they encourage healthy interaction and are played in moderation. God wants us to enjoy life, but He wants us to do so in a way that GLORIFIES Him!

Comment On This · Love This · Share with Friends

Pam: If most of your video game choices are filled with darkness, you cannot reasonably expect your inner soul to be filled with light.

Comment On This · Love This · Share with Friends

Yesterday at 4:43 pm

I heard that sexting is considered pornography. Is that true? I've been dating my boyfriend for a while, and he asked me to send him some racy pictures. I don't wan't to do anything wrong, but maybe that wouldn't be so bad.

Comment On This · Love This · Share with Friends

October 13 at 6:51 pm

My pastor said that pornography would not only harm us and our relationships with our future spouses, but also our relationships with God. I didn't have the guts to ask how. Can you explain?

Comment On This · Love This · Share with Friends

Chapter 6

Pornography Addiction Is Worse Than Chocolate

Pam: When you unleash the power of pornography, your brain chemistry will change, triggering a hazardous dependency, warped self-image and damaged relationships.

Comment On This · Love This · Share with Friends

Landon: Harsh words for what amounts to nothing more than tasteless pictures.

Comment On This · Love This · Share with Friends

Colby: Tasteless pictures? Really, man? I think they are a beautiful display of the beauty God made in the human body.

Comment On This · Love This · Share with Friends

Cassie: Wow. Wow. Wow. As a woman, let me chime in here. These aren't "beautiful displays of the beauty God made in the human body"! They are demeaning images of the "ideal" (but not normal) body and reduce women to animals. A "bunny"—really? Last I checked, God never referred to me as a bunny!

Comment On This · Love This · Share with Friends

Zach: I think it's a good alternative to sex for those of us with raging hormones.

Comment On This · Love This · Share with Friends

Micah: I thought that too, but somehow my "good alternative" has me feeling like my relationship with God has gotten very distant— so I'm not really sure it is a "good" alternative after all.

Comment On This · Love This · Share with Friends

Greg: I appreciate what you are doing to educate people about the value of the human body. For many years, I struggled with pornography. Because this was years ago, I couldn't get it in secret. I had to go into a store and purchase it, so other people knew what I was doing, and there was some shame in that. I knew it wasn't a tasteful thing to do. Quite honestly, that shame helped me break free of the addiction. Today, pornography is way too easy to access. You can get it on your computers, phones and even cable TV with a sense of complete anonymity.

Comment On This · Love This · Share with Friends

 Pam: You are right that ease of accessibility to pornography is cause for increased concern. Since acquiring pornography takes so little effort, there are MANY people today who are closet pornography addicts. Time spent viewing these pictures and photos in private seems like "exciting fun" until the need consumes them and then, because they have done this in secrecy, they have no idea how to ask for help until they are in serious trouble.

Comment On This · Love This · Share with Friends

 Rachel: I am one of those people. I was working on a school paper, and a porn "pop-up" appeared on my computer. I closed the window, thinking nothing of it at the time, but I guess I was curious. Later I started checking into more pictures to see what they were, how they were posed and what they were about. Now, even though I would tell you I don't want to look at it, I find myself getting home from school, going to my room and looking at it . . . AGAIN. I can't seem to stop. My parents would be so upset if they knew the truth.

Comment On This · Love This · Share with Friends

 Pam: Rachel, you are not alone. Disgustingly, many pornography producers associate website and pop-up names with search terms that children and teens are likely to enter. For this reason, first exposure is often foisted upon you even though you never sought it out.

I know you are concerned about talking to your parents, but they love you and would want to help you break this craving NOW rather than have you sink deeper into sin. Please talk to them today. If you find it too difficult to talk to them directly, I would encourage you to seek out a trusted adult—maybe a teacher, a mentor or a youth leader—who might be able to help you tell your parents and get the support and assistance you need.

Comment On This · Love This · Share with Friends

Newsflash: The average teen spends 1 hour and 40 minutes per week browsing for pornography.[1]

Lydia: My mom just got me a new phone, and she chose the Apple iPhone because they have banned pornography from their systems. I think that is awesome, because I don't have to worry about offensive images popping up. It is great to see a big company taking a stand against a sick, money-hungry industry!

Comment On This · Love This · Share with Friends

 Pam: I couldn't agree more! No matter how much flack they catch for doing the right thing, I pray their executives always know it is WORTH it. Through that decision, they are protecting MANY. It's awesome! I pray that other major corporations will follow suit.

Comment On This · Love This · Share with Friends

 Maren: I heard that sexting is considered pornography. Is that true? I've been dating my boyfriend for a while, and he asked me to send him some racy pictures. We aren't having sex, and I don't want to do anything wrong, but maybe that wouldn't be so bad.

Comment On This · Love This · Share with Friends

Pam: First of all, I get the sense that you think because you have chosen not to have physical sex, this would be a safe alternative to make this boy happy while not actually "doing it." But you need to understand that sending him "racy pictures" will cause sexual arousal (that IS why he wants to see them).

God knew that exposing our bodies would INCREASE the desire for intimate acts. This is why God's Word exhorts us "not to awaken love until the time is right" (Song of Solomon 2:7, *NLT*). The "right" time is marriage. If you ignore this scriptural warning, send him pictures and induce this effect, how can you still expect him to respect a safe boundary when he is around you?! You can't. He will want to act on what you've "given" him already. Continue to practice purity of mind and body as a couple. DON'T INVITE TEMPTATION THROUGH SEXUAL IMAGERY. If he harasses you for that, DUMP HIM! You deserve better!

Furthermore, you need to recognize that once these pictures are out there, they are like toothpaste squeezed from the toothpaste tube. They can never be taken back! You have NO CONTROL over what the recipient of the pictures does with them, and that could lead to a miserable existence. In fact, I vividly recall the story of Jesse Logan back in 2009.[2] In case you are unfamiliar with her story, Jesse texted some nude photos to her boyfriend, thinking that was "safe." After some time, they broke up, and the boy sent the photos on to some of Jesse's high school class-mates. As you can imagine, they started calling her horrific names, making walking through the hallways each day an ordeal. Dejected and overwhelmed, Jesse took matters into her own hands and ended the harassment by ending her life—at only 18 years old. Jesse's life ended far too soon because of real consequences to sexting.

Beyond that, it IS child pornography to send and/or receive these texts. While individual states have started to look at and vote on these laws, sexting is currently a felony according to federal law. This has led to many teens being charged and put on sex offender lists for mistreating their phones.[3,4,5,6] Be wise and NEVER sext!

Comment On This · Love This · Share with Friends

@ Link: Those who take, send AND receive sexting messages break laws. The news story at the link below was extremely powerful in communicating the SERIOUSNESS of sexting, which can result in child pornography charges. The three girls who took and sent the pictures are only 14 and 15 years old, and they are being charged with manufacturing, disseminating and possessing child pornography. The 16- and 17-year-old boys who received the sext messages are being charged with possession of child pornography. These are young teenagers who may have a criminal record, all because they thought they were having some "fun." Read the article and THINK about your own personal choices! http://www.wpxi.com/news/18469160/detail.html

Zoey: I had NO IDEA you could get in so much trouble for this. I mean, I know tons of people who have sexted on their phones. THANKS for the 411!

Comment On This · Love This · Share with Friends

Aryanna: A lot of times it seems that people kind of expect this in a relationship. I have to admit, it's nice to know this. It provides an easy "out."

Comment On This · Love This · Share with Friends

Pam: First of all, you should NEVER feel like you need an OUT to avoid doing something you don't want to do in a relationship. If a person is asking you to compromise your morals and clear boundaries, then they clearly do not care about you. They are trying to USE you to meet selfish desires. You deserve better. DON'T compromise! Remember that sexts are a permanent mark—a tattoo of sorts. Once they are sent, they are "out there." Keep what is yours—your body—for you and your spouse only!

Comment On This · Love This · Share with Friends

Newsflash: One in five teens has sent or posted nude/semi-nude pictures or videos of themselves.[7]

Stacy: I am very into text sex and will do it once a day with sometimes more than one guy. I know it's bad, but I enjoy it so much. What should I do?
Comment On This · Love This · Share with Friends

 Pam: Text sex, like actual physical sex, is a choice. You can say yes or you can say no. It is important that you say NO and stop the behavior, because if you allow it to continue, you will suffer. Your most important "sex organ" has nothing to do with the genital area. It is your mind. If you are filling your mind with hook-ups and illicit sex, you are permanently damaging the most important element of your sexuality and diminishing your ability to bond with one partner. DECIDE today that you will not continue to damage your mind this way and STICK TO IT. In the process, I bet you'll find that you have more respect for yourself and the people around you.
Comment On This · Love This · Share with Friends

 Samantha: I've been texting this guy lately, and he is asking me to do things with him like send pornographic pictures. When I told him that I did not want to and wouldn't do it, he got all mad at me. What do I do?
Comment On This · Love This · Share with Friends

 Pam: STOP COMMUNICATING with this guy, PERIOD. NO boy that cares about you would put you at risk and/or pressure you into behaviors that you have CLEARLY told him you will not do.

PLEASE UNDERSTAND that you should never be asked to be seen naked or have ANY kind of genital contact outside of marriage, because those interactions will place you at risk for physical, emotional and spiritual consequences that can be COMPLETELY avoided in healthy relationships. Tell him you don't appreciate the lack of respect, and that you want to quit communicating with him. If he continues to badger you, please tell your parents, a school official or someone else who can help end the behavior.
Comment On This · Love This · Share with Friends

 Pam: Pornography dehumanizes and devalues people.
Comment On This · Love This · Share with Friends

Lincoln: I've always thought of it as just fantasizing about people and sexual situations.

Comment On This · Love This · Share with Friends

 Pam: Hardly. Pornography warps your idea of the VALUE of people—made in the image of God—and reduces them to OBJECTS to be used to meet your own insatiable need. Women become simply BODY PARTS, and men become simply VEHICLES to make us feel wanted, desired and satisfied. We don't care about THE PEOPLE. It's unnecessary to have "relationships" or even know their names—they are simply commodities.

Comment On This · Love This · Share with Friends

 Bradley: I can see how this would be true. I have looked at porn before, and I found myself thinking that there was a "script" to sex. Then, when I was at church, and the pastor was talking about the beauty and intimate expression God created sex to be, I felt super convicted. My perspective had gotten so messed up. I knew I needed to stop looking at porn so that I could view women properly and experience sex (in marriage) as God designed it to be.

Comment On This · Love This · Share with Friends

 Kim: This discussion brings Psalm 119:37 to mind: "Turn my eyes away from worthless things; preserve my life according to your word."

Comment On This · Love This · Share with Friends

 Paul: How do you think this idea of sex is so different from the real deal?

Comment On This · Love This · Share with Friends

 Pam: God designed sex to be a physical, emotional and spiritual experience. God also blessed marital union (sex) to accomplish an incredible task: procreation. God is not anti-sex. He is PRO-SEX, but He means for it to be an experience that draws us nearer to Christ and binds us to one another—anything less than that is a cheap replacement of His best.

Pornography separates sex from one of its primary purposes—procreation—and reduces the sex act to mere self-indulgent recreation. There is no healthy emotional bond. It is NOT about love—selflessly giving up one's needs and desires for the other. It is about SELFISHLY using someone to meet your own needs.

Further, by reducing the other to mere body parts, pornography sets up false expectations about "real" women (and men), replacing actual human beings with doctored images. MOST women (or men for that matter) will not fit this mold; as a result, many people struggle with poor self-image and unhealthy ideas about the human body. At the same time, those looking at pornography are increasingly drawn to body parts rather than to the heart and soul of the other person.

In the "real deal," you aren't drawn to your spouse because of his or her physique, but because of who he or she is as a PERSON. Because you have fallen in love with your husband's or wife's HEART, the intimate expression of sex is profoundly beautiful. Because you have committed to love this one person properly, through good times and bad, and vowed never to leave them, the expression of sex is NOT an act of taking and using, but one of loving freely, totally, faithfully and fruitfully.[8]

Comment On This · Love This · Share with Friends

 Newsflash: "25 percent of search engine requests are pornography-related."[9]

 Pam: Denying the addictive potential of pornography is like denying the existence of gravity. It's been proven by science.
Comment On This · Love This · Share with Friends

> **Dayne:** For real?
> Comment On This · Love This · Share with Friends

> **Pam:** Absolutely. One source says that pornography causes such a powerful "chemical bath in the brain" that "the endorphins released are 5 to 7 times MORE addictive than cocaine" (emphasis added).[10] Drugs have long been acknowledged to be addictive, but it isn't popular to talk about pornography or its addictive nature. The silence must stop, and the truth must be told!
> Comment On This · Love This · Share with Friends

> **Tyler:** I believe it. A few years ago, I made a huge mistake. I started looking at pornography. I'm only 18, but now it seems like I almost can't go a week without having lustful thoughts, which 99 percent of the time end up in masturbation. When that happens, I feel distant from God, and all of my relationships suffer.
> Comment On This · Love This · Share with Friends

89

Pam: Thank you for being honest. It makes sense that you feel distant from God when you choose to look at pornography, have these thoughts and practice masturbation. These actions take the focus off of purity and place it on IMMEDIATE self-gratification. This goes DIRECTLY against God's design for healthy sexual activity and will make it more difficult to honor a NO GENITAL CONTACT boundary when you date someone, because you are used to getting what you want when you want it. Please seek out a Christian counselor, pastor or other trusted adult and get the help you need to break this addictive cycle.

Comment On This • Love This • Share with Friends

Alana: I spend hours on the Net and YouTube watching garbage. I never thought of it as an addiction or a bad thing, but now I'm thinking differently.

Comment On This • Love This • Share with Friends

✒ **Note: How Does Pornography Become an Addiction?** The brain's chemistry is affected when an individual views pornography. I found this explanation by Dr. Judith Reisman, an expert on this topic, helpful in understanding pornography's addictive power.

According to the field of neuropsychology, the brain has both excitatory and inhibitory transmitters, located in the right and left hemispheres of the brain, respectively, and the pornographic image triggers the former at the expense of the latter. Indeed, we now know that sexual imagery is more powerful and more indelible to the brain than even fear-inducing imagery.

Pornography thus causes our inhibitory transmitters to shut down, allowing the right brain, which is responsible for our emotional reflexes (lust, fear, shame, etc.), to override the logical left-brain activities that maintain control—homeostasis—in the body. This disrupts the entire process of human cognition and health. In fact, what we are looking at are erototoxins restructuring the human brain. The brain actually changes to accommodate the stimuli it experiences. . . .

Erototoxic materials trigger testosterone and endorphins. We actually get a high from sexual arousal. The big problem with this is that things that are vile and associated with sex become, over time, more arousing than things that are loving. . . .

[Pornography] is a drug—a poly-drug, to be more precise. Pornography causes you to experience a broad spectrum of drugs that the human body automatically produces on its own. And it triggers them all in one shot. It also triggers the bonding chemical oxytocin, known as the "cuddle chemical" or the "love chemical," which is even more confusing to the body and causes arousal to increase even further. Erototoxins induce lust, fear, shame, and hostility, and these trigger an endogenous drug high (endogenous meaning a drug you produce internally) that the organism mislabels as sexual arousal because it doesn't know what else to label it.[11]

Ally: I've always gotten the message that pornography was okay for boys to look at, and I had started entertaining the idea of looking at it but didn't know if it was okay for girls. I had no idea it was bad or addictive.

Comment On This · Love This · Share with Friends

Pam: What might seem culturally acceptable or innocent or "controllable" will quickly become an ADDICTION. You need more and more. Soft pornography is no longer "enough," and people begin to desire more graphic, vulgar, hard-core pornography. As this happens, you "lose your NO." At this point, some people will KNOW that the behavior is hurting them or the people around them, and even recognize the consequences of their choice, but simply stopping is no longer an option. It takes difficult, intentional work to break the habit. DO NOT start, or you will get sucked in.

I'm reminded of a great poem:

The Flies and the Honey Pot
by Aesop

A jar of honey chanced to spill
Its contents on the windowsill
In many a viscous pool and rill.

The flies, attracted by the sweet,
Began so greedily to eat,
They smeared their fragile wings and feet.

With many a twitch and pull in vain
They gasped to get away again,
And died in aromatic pain.

Moral:
O foolish creatures that destroy
Themselves for transitory joy.[12]

I hope this helps!

Comment On This · Love This · Share with Friends

Ally: Yes! Totally! Thank you so much.

Comment On This · Love This · Share with Friends

Stacy's Story

It is painful for me to even try to write my story about the way pornography destroyed my life. The journey to healing has been painful and very long, and my experience has left me with scars that will not be completely healed until I get to heaven. I decided to share the story, hoping that if it helps even one young person to avoid all the pain I have been through, then maybe the suffering can be redeemed.

My journey into pornography and sexual involvement with multiple partners began somewhat innocently, at least in my own mind, but I have come to see that NO amount of sexual impurity is innocent—ever. At about age 13, I started reading romance novels. My mom hid them in her closet, and I stumbled on them one day while I was "snooping"—trying to find a birthday present I was sure she had already bought. I found a stash of books, all worn, with covers that showed women with massive cleavage being embraced by "ripped," handsome men. I took one, pretty sure my mom would never notice it was missing. I hid the book under my bed in a shoebox, and I would take it out at night and read the most vivid descriptions of sex, filled with incredible detail. I began to need more. I replaced the first book I took with a different one, knowing that if I only took one at time, my mom would never notice.

When I was 16, I got a computer for my birthday, and my dad built a little desk in a cubby hole in my bedroom—perfect privacy. Now I had access not just to words on a page, but also to PICTURES and even videos! I was hooked. Pretty soon, just looking at pornography wasn't exciting enough. I had to move on to chat rooms and actually writing my own story with an anonymous person on the other side of a screen name. The sex talk got more and more involved, and soon they were sending me pictures of themselves having sex, and I reciprocated. It didn't take long for the "fake" stuff to become boring and not satisfying; I needed the real thing. I knew I didn't want a relationship—I was the good girl, who got good grades, who didn't date and who went to church. To everyone around me, I appeared to be making all the right choices. I wanted the sex to be completely anonymous with no strings attached. I didn't want to know his real name, and I certainly wasn't going to tell him mine. I began these hook-ups right after I started college. I can't even count the number. The adrenaline rush was amazing. I think I believed that sex would be different some day—when I actually wanted to have a "relationship"—and that I could sweep all of these encounters under the rug. I always made sure the guy used condoms, and I was taking birth control pills, so I thought all my bases were covered.

How wrong I was! My addiction started getting in the way of ALL normal relationships, not just dating relationships (which were nonexistent), but also friendships. I barely even spoke to my roommate. Then one day I woke up with incredible pain in my lower abdomen and genital region. I was so scared; it was like nothing I had ever

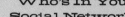
experienced before. The next day, I broke out with the most painful open sore—I could barely sit down or walk. I went to the campus health clinic and heard the words, "You have herpes." I just sat in shock. I had to get a prescription for the pain and sores, and then I needed further tests. Over the next few weeks, I learned that I had abnormal cells on my cervix, and that I had cancer that had already advanced to my uterus. Within six months, I had a complete hysterectomy and found myself back at home, having to face my parents. The world that I had kept hidden came crashing down.

I remember hearing the verse, "You may be sure that your sin will find you out" (Numbers 32:23), but I never imagined how painful that truth would be. I am now seeing a Christian counselor; I am a recovering sex addict. I finally confessed the sin—all of it, even the seemingly innocent "romance novel" addiction in junior high—knowing that it wasn't innocent at all; it led me down a path of almost complete destruction. Today, I am thankful for the forgiveness I have in Christ, but I know that I will have to fight this battle until I get to heaven. And I will bear the scar of my sin in my body for the rest of my life. Every time I take the medication to help my still young body deal with a hysterectomy, every time I have to tell someone I date about my past, and every time I face the truth that I will never be able to have children, I am reminded that sin ALWAYS has a consequence.

 Brett: My friends pressured me into my problem. When I was over at one of their houses one day, the guys put a bunch of porn on my laptop—and now I'm addicted to it. I don't want to have this addiction. I have a girlfriend, and this has changed how I see her. I have it in my heart to love my girlfriend for who she is, but I just can't seem to control my impure thoughts. She doesn't know about this problem, and I'm trying to stamp it out before it becomes a major concern to me, but I'm having a really hard time. HELP!

Comment On This · Love This · Share with Friends

 Pam: Pornography is incredibly destructive because unlike other drug addictions—like cocaine or nicotine (and understand I am NOT saying those addictions are okay!)—which will eventually flush from your system, pornography is essentially burned into your brain. Visually and mentally, it DOESN'T leave you. In fact, "Brain scientists tell us that 'in 3/10 of a second a visual image passes from the eye through the brain, and whether or not one wants to, the brain is structurally changed and memories are created—we literally "grow new brain cells" with each visual experience.'"[13]

It is important that you QUIT looking at pornography and get some good Christian counseling to help you break the addiction as well as regain respect for women and restore your relationship with Christ. These twisted images and ideas have certainly broken your relationship with Him. Until that is restored, and you once again recognize and honor intimacy as He created it, you will NOT be able to have a healthy dating relationship.

Telling your girlfriend is important. Honesty is a cornerstone of any godly marriage, and if you can't be honest with her about your shortcomings now, what makes you think you will be a man of integrity and be honest with her later? Will she break up with you? Maybe. I don't know. But she deserves the best, and you are not providing her the ability to be in a relationship where she can feel comfortable and safe when you hide important truths from her. Tell her today!

Comment On This · Love This · Share with Friends

Brett: I was afraid you'd say that.

Comment On This · Love This · Share with Friends

Lynn: I was on Pam's page and saw your post. As a girl who is in a relationship with a guy who's been addicted to pornography for nine years and JUST told me after two years of dating, TELL HER! My boyfriend told me it wasn't the images that he was after, and we are working on forgiveness. We've started going to couple's counseling, because as much as I want to, it is hard for me to overlook this history and trust him. I find myself checking up on him a lot. He's trying really hard, and I know that he thinks I'm the only one for him, but before we can marry we have to solidly work through this. Our biggest problem now is trying to stay sexually pure, both physically and mentally. Your girlfriend deserves a choice just like you do, and you need professional assistance, because if you don't get help, this addiction will follow you.

Comment On This · Love This · Share with Friends

📰 **Newsflash:** Every second, an average of 28,258 Internet users are viewing pornography.[14]

@ **Link:** Many of you are confessing (or just realizing) that you have a pornography addiction you need help breaking. I encourage you to check out www.pureintimacy.org for excellent resources as well as help finding a trustworthy counselor in your area.

Pam: "The face is the mirror of the mind, and eyes without speaking confess the secrets of the heart" (Saint Jerome). What is done in secret will come to light (see Luke 8:17).

Comment On This · Love This · Share with Friends

 John: To what extent do you believe pornography has an effect on marriage?

Comment On This · Love This · Share with Friends

 Pam: Pornography damages your ability to EVER experience true intimacy and sex the way God intended it to be. Marriage is meant to be the complete uniting of TWO valuable people—created in His image—to love each other fully. When you look at pornography, you bring THOSE people (even if they are just images burned into your brain) into your marriage bed. You are no longer "faithful" to your spouse. Your marriage bed is no longer pure. It is filled with countless others—even if they are just in your mind. Pornography is a twisted, cheap imitation of the gift of sex that God intended to reflect HIS love for you!

Comment On This · Love This · Share with Friends

 Reece: My pastor said that pornography would not only harm us and our relationships with our future spouses, but also our relationships with God. I didn't have the guts to ask how. Can you explain?

Comment On This · Love This · Share with Friends

 Pam: Yes, if you allow yourself to look at pornography, your relationship with God WILL suffer. You can't turn your back on His design and expect any other result. As our Creator, He gives us instructions for how, when and where we are to enjoy intimacy. If we ignore these instructions and misuse our bodies, we are setting ourselves and our spouses up for pain. Oftentimes, this leads to a hardened heart and anger towards God (*Why are You ruining my fun and making me feel bad about myself?*), so individuals turn their backs on Him. Now, the one person—our Savior—capable of providing true healing to the individuals and the marriage has been taken out of the equation, leaving couples weaker and more susceptible to a failed relationship. This is hardly the picture of the "perfect" way to wait. The perfect way to wait is by REFUSING to look at anything vile and honoring a NO GENITAL CONTACT boundary until you marry!

Comment On This · Love This · Share with Friends

Newsflash: 47% of Christians report pornography being "a major problem in the home."[15]

💜 Carl's Story

When I was in high school, I got a computer in my room. Today I would call this a problem. To any other teenager out there with a computer in your room, I encourage you to move it. Mine got me into trouble, and I know that I'm not alone.

After my parents would go to bed, I'd get online, and pornography pop-ups would appear. I started looking at the images more closely and having the urge to look at them again and again. I tried to tell myself that what I was doing was wrong and not to look again, but I would fail. Even while I was looking at it, I knew it was wrong.

I'm Catholic. One night, I was hanging with my youth group, and the topic of discussion was pornography. Honestly, I played it cool, like I didn't look at it and didn't know why people would, but inside my stomach was churning. Our leader talked about pornography's effect on marriage, and I had a more intense feeling of regret. What was I doing? What kind of guy was I that I was already wrecking my future marriage?

I wanted out, so I decided to confess to my parents. They were über-disappointed. They couldn't believe it, and my mom cried. I knew what I'd done must be really hurtful to women when I saw her crying. But they thanked me for being honest with them and put some filters on the computer in an attempt to stop the addictive behavior.

Soon after this incident, I started college. I was a computer science major, which was not good for a person struggling with a computer-related addiction. When I went to my parents' house, I could get around any pornography-blocking program they had installed. Don't get me wrong—I really did want to stop, but I was compulsive.

I met my girlfriend that same year. She was a beautiful woman of God—the type every guy dreams of. She was a virgin. She wanted to be a nurse and help people. She volunteered a ton, and every time I looked at her, I knew God must be pleased with who she was and her choices in life. I didn't have the same feeling about myself, because my head wasn't filled with faith and charity. It was consumed by this one question: "Would sex with her be like it looked on all those computer videos?" I was defiling her innocence in my head.

I knew I was in big trouble, so I told her what was going on, and then I went to confession. Just admitting what a scumbag I was before God actually felt good. Then I started to meet weekly with a Christian counselor. He helped me get more into the Word of God, and between his counsel and the help of my priest, I am happy to say that I turned my life around.

I was particularly impacted by Galatians 5:16-18. Paul says, "So I say, walk by the Spirit, and you will not gratify the desires of the flesh. For the flesh desires what is contrary to the Spirit, and the Spirit what is contrary to the flesh. They are in conflict with each other, so that you are not to do whatever you want. But if you are led by the Spirit, you are not under the law." When we say we believe in Christ, and His Spirit comes into our lives, it puts to death living by the flesh. Did I want to really be a believer and walk in the Spirit? I had a choice. We ALL have a choice. I could submit to God and walk in His ways, or I could live by the ways of the world. I choose to live in

His will. I choose to let Him—rather than my flesh—be my authority. In the process, He has molded me into a man that I am proud to be.

📖 **Note: The Sin Cycle.** "But each person is tempted when they are dragged away by their own evil desire and enticed. Then, after desire has conceived, it gives birth to sin; and sin, when it is full-grown, gives birth to death" (James 1:14-15).

I was listening to Casting Crowns' song "Slow Fade" and was reminded again of how easy it is to fall—and fall hard—when we don't pay attention to the so-called little sins in our lives. People never wake up in the morning and say, "I think I will ruin my life today" or "Maybe today I will destroy my marriage, hurt my children and make sure that I experience excruciating pain for the next decade." The little compromises along the way—the ones we think don't matter—are what cause us to end up sitting in the mud with pigs, filthy and starving, wondering how we got here from the mansion in which we were raised (see Luke 15:11-19).

James describes the "sin cycle" so clearly in chapter 1 of his epistle. We are all "dragged away by [our] own evil desire and enticed." Some translations use the term "lust," which can be defined as "fulfilling a natural and good DESIRE with ANYTHING that God has not provided to meet that desire." Desires for sex and intimacy are NOT wrong. In fact, they are God-given! But God also gave a very specific boundary so that these desires could be filled perfectly, without hurting yourself or anyone else—and that boundary is marriage. When we decide to fulfill our desires with sex outside of marriage—even with "images" of sex outside of marriage—we are filling our desires selfishly and telling God that we are going to take care of things our OWN way, thank you very much.

At this point what is "conceived" in our lives is "sin." You might not even know it is embedded in your soul, but it will grow and grow—and when SIN comes to full term, what comes out of your life is DEATH. The Greek word in this verse does not mean that your soul gives birth to something that is DEAD. It actually means that what comes out of your soul is very much alive, but it will KILL everything it touches. Eventually this "sin" in the depth of your soul that you have hidden from everyone—this sin that you thought no one saw, and maybe even justified and hid from YOURSELF—will KILL you and all those around you! This is serious stuff! You have damaged yourself physically, emotionally and spiritually. We see evidence of this death all around us in disease, infidelity, adultery, and broken marriages and families.

How do I make sure that I am not harboring "lust" and that sin has not taken root in my soul? David wrote in the Psalms, "Search me, O God, and know my heart; test me and know my anxious thoughts. Point out anything in me that offends you, and lead me along the path of everlasting life" (Psalm 139:23-24, *NLT*).

Have you asked God to do these things for you? Please take some time right now to quiet yourself before God. Ask the Holy Spirit to reveal to you any sin that might be lurking in your soul, just waiting to be unleashed in your life. Confess that sin before God. Scripture says that if we confess our sin, "He is faithful and just and will forgive us our sins and will purify us from all unrighteousness" (1 John 1:9). It also says that He throws our sin "as far as the east is from the west" (Psalm 103:12)!

Then you need to find others to help you take hold of these scriptural promises. James 5:16 says, "Confess your sins to each other and pray for each other so that you may be healed. The earnest prayer of a righteous person has great power and produces wonderful results" (*NLT*). It is important that you find someone you trust (a youth minister, pastor, mentor or other godly adult), with whom you can share your struggle, so that they can help you and hold you accountable. When our sins are kept secret, even if we confess them to God privately, it is very easy to fall back into the same pattern. When someone who loves us KNOWS about our struggle with this sin, they can lovingly ask us, "How are you doing? How can I pray for you?" None of us is strong enough to fight the battle against sin alone. We need one another's help.

Hunter: I think that it is time I quit this habit. Thanks for the help!

Comment On This • Love This • Share with Friends

Nora: I accidentally found a pornographic magazine when I was eight. I started getting into all kinds of pornography and even sex until a couple of years ago, when I realized it was wrong. I was out of control. Then I finally told God what I was feeling bad about and told my youth leader. I feel much better today.

Comment On This • Love This • Share with Friends

Owen: I'm 15 and I started watching pornography a few years ago. I have felt ashamed the whole time, because I know it's wrong, but I didn't know how to stop. Thanks so much for giving me the exact steps necessary to break this lifestyle.

Comment On This • Love This • Share with Friends

Pam: You are welcome! Another GREAT resource for you is *Every Young Man's Battle*[16] by Stephen Arterburn (for females, there is *Every Young Woman's Battle*[17]). Please be sure to check it out. I pray that you will allow Jesus to redeem all that has brought pain and darkness to your life!

Comment On This • Love This • Share with Friends

Pam: Today you have a choice. Be dependent on Christ and live life to the fullest, or be dependent upon pornography, ruining your present and risking your future. I hope you will choose God's design!

Comment On This • Love This • Share with Friends

Chapter 7

I Think I Look Like a Model—Facebook Is Feeding My Ego!

 Pam: Social networking sites offer wonderful opportunities to communicate with others, but they don't come without risk. Being wise about how you use them is critical, as is being aware of how they can affect your relationships, safety and overall health!

Comment On This · Love This · Share with Friends

 Tony: I love Facebook! It allows me to track some people's lives that I otherwise wouldn't be able to.

Comment On This · Love This · Share with Friends

 Danielle: I went off to college, and having Myspace and Facebook pages keeps me in touch with my high school friends.

Comment On This · Love This · Share with Friends

 Jordan: My friends and I make pretty much all of our plans via Facebook. It's way easier than making a bunch of phone calls.

Comment On This · Love This · Share with Friends

 Sara: Tweet. Tweet. Anyone on Twitter?

Comment On This · Love This · Share with Friends

 Laura: Twitter rocks. I can put whatever I'm thinking out there into cyberland and get it off my mind without being that much of a "person" to whoever follows me. It's just like a stream of a bunch of people's thoughts and opinions.

Comment On This · Love This · Share with Friends

 Tracy: That has gotten me into trouble. Sometimes I'll want to get stuff off of my mind, and I'll post things without thinking.

Comment On This · Love This · Share with Friends

📰 **Newsflash:** 73% of teens with Internet access use social networking sites.[1]

Connor: One of the oddest things I use Facebook for is homework help. I really like it because there are people to "talk" to about my assignments all the time. On the other hand, it seems really weird. I mean, it kind of seems like studying together should be a face-to-face thing.

Comment On This · Love This · Share with Friends

 Pam: The advent of online social networking has created new ways of communicating with one another. There are many pros to this because it does provide a way to communicate with people at all times, the ability to share things of value to you, and an opportunity to encourage your friends who may be struggling (even if they're geographically far away from you). It CAN be a ministry.

However, this new way of communicating is not without risks. You really have to work on keeping a balance between online communication and actual "face-to-face" relationship time. You have to figure out who you should "friend" and who you shouldn't. You have to determine whom you will instant message with or talk to in chat rooms. You have to be careful to recognize that people might not always represent themselves honestly, and that the person someone claims to be online may have nothing to do with who he or she really is. You have to acknowledge that the things you post about another person could hurt them, and that the things you post about yourself are now on display for the whole world—permanently.

Social networking is a responsibility. Take some time to pray and think hard about how you are using it and the people who are in your network. This will help you bring honesty into your own "networking world" and hopefully bring peace into your life, whether you are doing homework or just chatting back and forth.

Comment On This · Love This · Share with Friends

 Janna: One of my biggest beefs with social networking is that some of my closest friends don't pick up the phone and call anymore. We've gotten so lazy that we just write on each other's walls or text; we never actually call to make plans or send mail or anything. If we didn't see each other in school, it'd all be a virtual relationship (minus get-togethers that we plan online), and these are my so-called best friends.

Comment On This · Love This · Share with Friends

 Pam: This is an interesting challenge that we are all struggling with. Quick, easy and convenient communication suddenly supersedes close bonding and one-on-one discussion. The key is

TALKING to your friends about how you are feeling, since this is obviously affecting you and your relationships. Just like you want them to talk to you, you need to talk to them.

Comment On This · Love This · Share with Friends

📝 **Note: Are You Substituting the "Superficial" for What Is REAL?** When God created the world and then man, He knew immediately that it wasn't good for man to be alone—so He created woman to be man's wife, friend and partner in the world (see Genesis 2:18-24). From the beginning, God created us IN COMMUNITY.

Social networking makes it possible for people to replace "quality time" spent in community—actually listening to the other, being heard and hearing with more than just our ears—with "one way" (and one-dimensional) communication. There is great potential for misunderstanding in this type of communication. When you say something to someone face to face, they are able to observe your inflection and body language to help them know whether the statement is made seriously or in jest, for instance. The same exact words could be taken completely differently when they appear in a comment on a status or as a tweet. Finding a real balance between online communication and face-to-face time building authentic relationships can be tricky.

My friend Jan Kern, author of several books about breaking free from addiction and deception, has some valuable insights to share with all of us. I hope this excerpt helps you!

> To many people, constant Internet use is the "new normal," but author Jan Kern challenges this, asserting that too much Internet use is an addiction just like many others.
>
> While affirming that "God isn't anti-Internet," Kern argues that God wants more for us, wants us to have a real life and relationships, not just virtual ones.
>
> "The Internet can offer a really great experience, and for many people, this is not a problem. Most of us use the Internet for research, news, communication—and fun," said author Jan Kern.
>
> "But for some, it can easily become an obsession. Without realizing it, we get sucked into activities that rob us of the amazing identity, resources, and relationships God has in mind for us," she continued.
>
> "We can become so drawn in by the virtual satisfaction of our wants and desires that we miss the opportunity to see how God might meet those needs more fully in real life."[2]

 Michelle: Thank you for this! I always find it kind of funny when people say, "What would we do without cell phones? Without the Internet? Without computers?" I say to myself, *Well . . . what DID we do before all this?* These tools, both positive and negative, have just made our lives easier. It is easy to get info we need, easy to keep in touch, and easy to get things done more quickly. But, in the end, why does it matter if it's easy? We don't even realize we've been lost, meandering mindlessly through cyberspace with our eyes fixed on a screen as we type furiously, trying to stay "connected" before we run out of time.

Comment On This · Love This · Share with Friends

 Brittni: I was dating this guy for 2½ months, and I really fell for him. He was always saying the sweetest things. Everything was going well until this last weekend, when I told him something he didn't like, and we got in a fight. For a few days, he refused to answer my phone calls and gave me the cold shoulder. Then I got on my Facebook account and read, "Andrew and Brittni ended their relationship." He broke up with me over Facebook. I kind of think this is funny, because we just watched your video at youth group last night, and you mocked people breaking up with each other that way.

Comment On This · Love This · Share with Friends

 Pam: This is one KEY area where a computer conversation or status change can never substitute for healthy interaction. If you think of dating as a training ground for marriage, you want to make sure that you are able to talk and be honest with one another about everything. Marriage necessitates that. Computers should NEVER be used for these "heart" conversations.

Comment On This · Love This · Share with Friends

📰 **Newsflash:** Online social networking has become such a prime form of communication that 51% of teens admit to checking their sites more than once a day, and 22% check theirs more than 10 times a day.[3]

 Pam: "Time is free, but it's priceless. You can't own it, but you can use it. You can't keep it, but you can spend it. Once you've lost it you can never get it back" (Harvey MacKay).

Comment On This · Love This · Share with Friends

 Kami: That quote is like a sucker punch to the gut. When I get home from school, I spend tons of time on Myspace and YouTube. If I tracked the hours, it would be an embarrassing use of time in a day.

Comment On This · Love This · Share with Friends

Ian: I love Facebook and Twitter for communicating, whether it be with friends on Facebook or bands/artists that I follow on Twitter. However useful these sites may be, though, they also cause me great distraction. Like from my homework right now . . . ☺

Comment On This · Love This · Share with Friends

 Finley: BIG distraction. I could end up wasting a lot of time needed to work on other things. At the same time, social networking sites keep me in touch with people and help me stay informed about groups I like through their announcements.

Comment On This · Love This · Share with Friends

 Emily: I waste so much time on Facebook and Twitter it's unbelievable. I constantly update my pages. I also use Facebook to see what is going on in other people's lives—and, of course, something we all use it for: Facebook creeping.

Comment On This · Love This · Share with Friends

 Newsflash: "Facebook has more than 500 million registered users (Facebook 2010). If it were a country, it would have the third largest population in the world"![4]

 Taryn: I'm totally addicted to social media. It takes up a ton of my time every day. I have to check what my friends have posted, and I'm always intrigued by Twitter—seeing what people are saying and finding out if any new people are following me. And YouTube . . . well, don't get me started. Someone's always telling me about some new video I need to check out, and of course I do. My grades are suffering, and my parents are ticked off. They are not chill with my habits. What do I do?

Comment On This · Love This · Share with Friends

Pam: Look at your words. You RECOGNIZE your problem. You are spending TOO MUCH TIME online. My suggestion would be that you set new rules for yourself. How many hours do you need to spend, on average, doing homework each night? Once you answer that question, figure out the time that remains (given a reasonable bedtime), and allow a PORTION of that time to be spent with social media. Let's say you give yourself an hour. When the timer goes off, log out of all your sites and do your homework—all of it. If you finish and have some time left over, you can check your accounts again, but make sure that you are getting done what is most important FIRST. BEHAVIOR MODIFICATION is necessary for your life success right now. Don't let your future slip away over the computer!

Comment On This · Love This · Share with Friends

📧 **Newsflash:** Twitter users log 1,200 tweets per second.[5]

👉 **Note: Working for the Next Big Laugh?** I meet them every day: students in my audiences who are the "wanna be" comedians of their schools. Give me a couple of minutes up front with a mic, and I can tell you who is craving the attention of their peers.

YouTube and other video blogging networks have given anyone with access to the Internet the opportunity to broadcast themselves, or other sorts of video content, over the Internet. People who are trying to be "the next big thing" often fall into this trap. As a society, we have become obsessed with filming our every waking moment in order to show them to the world. Unfortunately, in the race to become the next YouTube sensation, some are putting their very lives at risk to get attention.

Although most posting is harmless fun, there are certainly risks lurking behind each click of the mouse. Beyond the obvious issues of sexual themes, bad language, bullying and all-around stupidity, there is the very real danger that we are wasting our lives looking for the next big laugh.

 Alan: You can totally tell that some people record stuff thinking it's funny, but I wonder if they ever look back at it later and think, *Well, that was dumb*. The sad thing is that I heard future employers look at YouTube posts and Facebook profiles and stuff, and then the things that were just wasting time suddenly become deal breakers.

Comment On This · Love This · Share with Friends

 Jeremiah: I laugh at how scripted life has become. Sometimes it is like people just have a camera going all the time for those moments that could make a good clip. It doesn't even seem natural.

Comment On This · Love This · Share with Friends

 Pam: Whether it is natural or not, it IS important that people are THINKING. Just because it is easy to post things on YouTube or Facebook or Myspace doesn't mean that a person should. You're right, Alan, employers are looking at these sites, so it is important that everything you post truly reflect the character you want people to see in you!

Comment On This · Love This · Share with Friends

📧 **Newsflash:** More than 24 hours of video are uploaded to YouTube every minute.[6]

Pam: Before you post anything on a social networking site, do you ask yourself, "How will this impact my reputation?"
Comment On This · Love This · Share with Friends

 Camdyn: Admittedly, I'm sometimes too spontaneous. I just post.
Comment On This · Love This · Share with Friends

 Aubrey: Facebook is a glorified email account complete with a soapbox to make public announcements.
Comment On This · Love This · Share with Friends

 Pam: Having the opportunity to share our ideas can be a wonderful thing, but if it is done too spontaneously without thought, it does become a soapbox complete with risk of harming oneself or others. You MUST THINK before you ACT (or post or hit the "upload" button)!
Comment On This · Love This · Share with Friends

 Lacey: Good advice. When I was 13, my parents let me open a Facebook account. I was young and not particularly thoughtful. When my girlfriends and I hit up the beach one afternoon, we took tons of pictures, because that's just what we do. They weren't "naughty," but we were in bikinis. I didn't think anything of posting them, but then I got to school and a bunch of the guys were like, "Hey, Lacey, lookin' good!" or "Will you wear your bikini to school? Love the eye candy!" Some might like that kind of attention, but I HATED it.
Comment On This · Love This · Share with Friends

Pam: We all love to go to the beach or pool, but what we wear at the beach or pool is not appropriate attire for every situation (just picture yourself going to church in your swimwear!). So, posting pictures of yourself or your friends in bikinis on a public site might not be a great idea. If you do, that becomes the image of you that boys carry in their heads (even if that wasn't your intention). Then, when you go to school, you no longer get the respect you want, because they look at you and see the picture of you in their heads instead.
Comment On This · Love This · Share with Friends

📱 **Newsflash:** "22% of teens . . . say they are personally more forward and aggressive using sexually suggestive words and images [via technology] than they are in 'real life.'"[7]

💬 Marcie's Story

One night I went to a school play with some girl-friends. One of my friends introduced me to this guy, Jared, and that night he found me on Facebook. I felt comfortable "friending" him because we'd met in person. He and I are both online a lot, so we would IM (instant message). We started talking about random things like life, school, parents, teachers, etc. One night he asked me if I was scared to act sexually with a boy. I haven't had sex, but I also thought he was cool and didn't want him to think that I was lame, so I just said that I wasn't. Nothing more.

Well, we were at a game one time, and he told me that he thought I was scared. Looking back, he was being totally manipulative. He was just messing with my head, but I thought he really sensed my innocence. So, I set out to prove to him that I wasn't scared, and that was TOTALLY WRONG OF ME!!! We went for a walk and talked about the IMs. I KNEW I wasn't going to "do it," but I did start making out with him. Then he pulled me in closer and told me that he "wanted more."

I freaked out and told him no. He got super mad and started asking me why I spent all this time acting one way on the computer and then a different way in person. I didn't really have a good answer. To make it worse, later he told my friend the whole ENTIRE story. He repeated all the stuff I'd said in our IM chats and told her how it turned out, and then they both thought less of me—he because I didn't actually want to give it up, and she because she couldn't believe I would be so fake behind the screen. I learned my lesson. Now I only post pure things, and I stick to my values. My reputation is at stake every time I am online!

 Nisha: I live in a boring small town where there are seriously no cool guys. Recently I met the nicest guy on the Internet that I could ever possibly meet. My parents don't really like it; they say he is a stranger, and that makes it dangerous. I think they just don't get the new way to meet new people and date. I mean, he looks super sweet in his profile picture, and he's my age, and he always knows what to say. I'm trying to figure out a way to MEET him because he's that amazing. We totally have a connection.

Comment On This · Love This · Share with Friends

 Pam: First of all, you must be watching WAY TOO MUCH of *The Bachelor*. The contestants on that show always have an incredible "connection" to some guy they don't genuinely know, and he is always carrying on exactly the same flirtatious way with other girls, both on and off the show. What are the chances this boy is doing the same?

Remember, people can be WHOEVER they want from behind a screen. A 40-year-old can be 16. A rapist can be your best friend.

Online predators are real. In fact, just recently a 28-year-old post-man created eight different Facebook and Bebo profiles. Apparently he looked "super sweet" in his fake profiles and "always knew what to say" too, because he groomed up to 1,000 preteens and teens for sex. Just like you are thinking the boy you've "connected" with could be without fault, obviously this predator's virtual friends thought the same of him. Over time, he built their trust and made plans to meet, but it didn't turn out anything like the fairy tale in your mind. He sexually abused the young people who trusted him, shattering their lives.[8]

Sadly, this isn't an isolated incident. Cases like this happen every day. A 10-year-old boy was the target of child pornographers on YouTube. He thought he was posting nude pictures for some 14-year-old girls he'd met online, but his new "friends" were actually online predators.[9] Two teen girls were killed in connection to Myspace predators.[10] The list goes on and on.

This is NOT to say that every person behind a computer screen is a fake or a sex predator. But it DOES mean that POTENTIAL exists with every person you do not know in real life. For this reason, it is important that you NOT friend or share information with anyone you don't know in your day-to-day life.

Please do not go rushing out to find Mr. Right. In God's time, He will reveal His plan and mate for you. For now, be safe so that you are AROUND to meet him!

Comment On This • Love This • Share with Friends

Mandy: Wow. There are some people on my friend list I haven't actually met, but have had ongoing conversations with. One invited me to her graduation party, so I've been assuming we aren't "stranger" status anymore. This makes me question going.

Comment On This • Love This • Share with Friends

Isaac: I decide to friend people when I feel like I trust them enough to give them my cell phone number. Maybe I shouldn't be giving that out so freely?!

Comment On This • Love This • Share with Friends

Pam: DEFINITELY not. Most social networking sites have privacy settings that you can set to block this info. I would STRONGLY encourage you to do so and be VERY CAREFUL in your own day-to-day life, chat rooms and other settings NOT to give it out so freely. Your cell phone provides DIRECT ACCESS to you!

Comment On This • Love This • Share with Friends

Katie: I only add people I know or want to get to know. I'm going to be a little more careful from now on. Your answer to Nisha freaked me out!

Comment On This • Love This • Share with Friends

 Newsflash: "14 percent of students in 10th-12th grade have accepted an invitation to meet an online stranger in-person and 14 percent of students, who are usually the same individuals, have invited an online stranger to meet them in-person."[11]

 Pam: "Character is always lost when a high ideal is sacrificed on the altar of conformity and popularity" (Unknown). Is what you're posting positive and uplifting, or are you putting others down to be funny or popular?

Comment On This • Love This • Share with Friends

 Trista: When I see that people are trying to start something with someone else, I block them because I don't want to be a part of it. I see a lot of cyber-bullying going on in the name of being "cool."

Comment On This • Love This • Share with Friends

 Daniel: Sometimes your friends will start harassing someone, and you jump in thinking it's all in good fun. It's only later, when you're in the principal's office or you hear that they are super depressed, that you realize it takes such a toll on people.

Comment On This • Love This • Share with Friends

 Brandy: One of my friends got a bunch of posts from a group of girls calling her a "whore" because they all wanted her boyfriend and were jealous. She was so embarrassed and mad that she broke up with him just to get rid of the problem. It's sad, because he was a really good guy, and their relationship shouldn't have ended over stupid girls.

Comment On This • Love This • Share with Friends

Jezebel: I'll 'fess up. I'm guilty of being part of the popular group that occasionally pumps ourselves up by picking on others' weaknesses. It's dumb, but it goes with the territory of being a teenager. My mom found out and is seriously ticked off. I'm trying to figure out how to keep my friends without reducing myself to hurting others in the name of being "cool."

Comment On This • Love This • Share with Friends

 Pam: If you are going along with your friends in hurting others, are these really the type of friends you want to have? Is this the kind of person you want to be?

Comment On This · Love This · Share with Friends

 John: I've been cyber-bullied and bullied to my face. For anyone out there feeling down because they are being victimized, please, please, PLEASE go to an adult before it's too late.

Comment On This · Love This · Share with Friends

 Pam: Good advice, John! Please be sure to tell a parent, counselor, youth pastor/priest, or someone you trust so that steps can be taken to protect you in the future.

Comment On This · Love This · Share with Friends

 Newsflash: "Three-fourths of American teenagers say they've been bullied online, but only one in ten tells their parents."[12]

Michelle: I've been cyber-bullied by someone I thought was a good friend. She keeps saying, "Watch your back. Teachers don't see everything." I'm pretty creeped out, but I've kept my mouth shut because I don't know what to do. Any advice?

Comment On This · Love This · Share with Friends

 Pam: I am glad you are reaching out for help. First of all, TELL YOUR PARENTS. Because I am a parent myself, I can tell you that your parents love you DEARLY and would want to be made aware of what is happening so that they can help protect you both physically and emotionally. Someone is doing something TO YOU. You are not responsible for this person's behavior, so you should not feel ashamed. Please talk to your mom and dad!

Since this person is obviously someone who goes to school with you and hasn't kept her identity anonymous, have your parents help you decide who would be the best school official to talk to about this as well. I know that you don't want to get anyone in trouble, but you cannot permit this form of harassment to continue. These DANGEROUS threats need to be taken seriously.

As far as helping on the social networking sites, I would say BLOCK anybody who cyber-bullies. Such a person is obviously not a true friend, so he or she doesn't need to be your "friend" online. Cyber-bullying is a SERIOUS, growing problem that you SHOULD NOT tolerate. Hope this helps!

Comment On This · Love This · Share with Friends

🐾 Jesse's Story

People cyber-bully all the time to be "cool," and it's terrible. People say so many hurtful things to other people. Half the time, you can't believe that people would actually say some of the stuff they do, but I think they feel more comfortable doing it because they are behind the screen of a computer rather than face to face. It's totally a cheap thing to do, but it is very powerful. I'm in high school and I've been harassed. I'm sure it will keep happening more frequently.

As much as everyone claims to hate it, they can sometimes be hypocrites. I've seen plenty of people say, "I hate it when people bully others," but then they turn around and tag-team with another bully instead of doing anything about the situation. People don't like admitting it, but it's true. You know how I know? Because even though I have been bullied and hate it and know how rotten it makes you feel, I've done the same thing to others. Computers just make it too easy.

Now I am trying to fully purify myself with a new, positive attitude. I'm working really hard to become a friendlier person by getting involved with community groups and my church. Maybe I can't stop other people from being cyber-bullies, but at least I can try to set a good example of how to treat others—online and in the "real" world."

@ **Link:** If you don't think cyber-bullying is a serious problem, please take a look at this video from a grieving father who now tours the nation speaking to preteens/teens on this very issue because his son committed suicide as a result of online bullying. His message is one that will make you think, and it also offers tremendous hope. http://www.youtube.com/watch?v=iDBiqUWRtMo

---

 Pam: New research suggests there is a link between Facebook and depression.[13] Have you noticed this in your own life?

Comment On This · Love This · Share with Friends

 Erin: I am obsessed, but I don't think it means depression. I think people log in just to see what others are up to or to check their notifications. My grades actually went up after I joined! Imagine that! I find it helpful to ask people questions I wouldn't normally ask. I think Facebook depression is when kids aren't on it, because that means they are having problems either on Facebook or at school. I have seen some photos and status updates that make me think twice about the people posting them, but at least they are expressing some emotion and accepting comments on it. Plus I think some people just do it for attention. Well, that's just my opinion as a teen!

Comment On This · Love This · Share with Friends

Joel: I can see how this could be true. When I post a status update, I find myself checking on my phone constantly to see if people are commenting on it. I definitely feel "cooler" when people do. If they don't, I feel like they are looking at it and just saying, "Oh, whatever," and that makes me feel like a loser.

Comment On This · Love This · Share with Friends

 Siri: I think people do sometimes post things for attention. There is a major problem if they have to post stuff on the web and see responses to feel like they have value.

Comment On This · Love This · Share with Friends

 Pam: GREAT point. Our value needs to come through recognizing our worth in the eyes of the Lord—NOT through affirmative comments on Facebook!

Comment On This · Love This · Share with Friends

 Philip: I think Facebook depression goes back to the amount of time spent online. Obviously if a person is spending a lot of time on the site, that shows that they put a lot of stock in what other people have to say over the computer about them or their posts. That probably wasn't the point of Facebook, but it is easy to get sucked into the trap. Everyone is on it, so you want to maintain a cool image. Personally, I found myself spending way too much time checking to see what people were writing about my stuff and about me, and it was dragging me down. I wasn't thinking enough about OTHER things. I'd encourage my peers to keep this in check, because otherwise I think it's possible to sink into depression before you realize you are on the downhill slide.

Comment On This · Love This · Share with Friends

 Pam: Thanks for speaking out and encouraging your peers, Philip!

Comment On This · Love This · Share with Friends

📝 **Note: Warning Signs of Facebook Depression.** Recently I had the privilege of meeting relationship expert Janie Lacy. She provided this excellent list of warning signals that you might be suffering from Facebook depression. Please look it over and make sure you CUT BACK or GET HELP if needed!

1. **Obsession:** You spend large amounts of time talking and thinking about your Facebook activity.

2. **Social Isolation:** You spend more time alone and engaging in online activity than in face-to-face time with your friends.

3. **Academic performance change:** You've gotten lower grades and have dedicated less time to studying than you did before.

4. **Physical appearance/health decline:** You're more fatigued than usual and/or appear to have a loss of energy nearly every day.

5. **Significant mood change over a short period of time:** You get sad or moody more frequently than in the past.

To learn more from Janie, please check out her website at www.JanieLacy.com.

 Aubrey: I saw a news story on this, and people were mocking it at school because parents were watching over their kids' shoulders and asking them, "How are you feeling?" but I think it would be hard for most of us to look at this list and not see at least one of the components in ourselves. It's worth the warning.

Comment On This · Love This · Share with Friends

 Heather: I get how it's a popularity contest. People compare number of "friends" and stuff, and you don't want to be the odd ball out that no one seems to care about—or worse yet gets made fun of. Lots of times, people post pictures from parties, and if you weren't invited you naturally feel bad. It all makes sense. The question is how much control we give our Facebook page over our emotions.

Comment On This · Love This · Share with Friends

 Pam: GREAT point!

Comment On This · Love This · Share with Friends

📝 **Note: Stewardship of Time.** "Time is limited, so I better wake up every morning fresh and know that I have just one chance to live this particular day right, and to string my days together into a life of action, and purpose" (Lance Armstrong).

Does my time—and how I spend it—really matter to God? We have seen how much time we spend on our online pursuits. Even though some of the activities we are undertaking online have a good purpose (homework, connection, communication, even teaching), it is so easy to lose ourselves, wasting the entire afternoon or evening and being emotionally impacted by what we have seen.

Now let me challenge you. How much time do you spend with God during an average week? If you aren't spending any of your "free" time with God, are you really

putting HIM first in your life? Jesus teaches that we cannot serve God and the world. We must choose one or the other. In Matthew 6:24, Jesus says, "No one can serve two masters. Either you will hate the one and love the other, or you will be devoted to the one and despise the other." However, that doesn't mean we must reject everything that's in the world. It's a question of priority. Jesus also says, "Seek first his kingdom and his righteousness, and all these things will be given to you as well" (Matthew 6:33). The specific "things" He's referring to are food, drink and clothing—material things that Christians and non-Christians alike need, want and enjoy.

My suggestion is to sit down and write out how much time you spend on average each week with God in prayer, Bible study, youth group or church. A person who goes to school 35 hours a week, sleeps 57 hours a week, and spends 25 hours a week doing chores, playing sports, doing homework and maybe working a part-time job or babysitting has 26 hours of discretionary time per week. What percentage of your free time do you think you spend with Him? What percentage of it do you really spend with Him?

Next list all the other activities that take up your free time. Is any one of your free-time activities more important than spending time with God? Can one of these activities save your soul? What do you think—If a person spends only 1 or 2 percent of their discretionary time with God, what does that say to God? If you take a vacation for two weeks every year (that's 224 hours of "me" time), but only spend 52 or perhaps 156 hours a year with God, what does that say to God?

I am not suggesting that ALL of your "me" time should be spent in a formal way with God. God did give us all things to enjoy (see 1 Timothy 6:17). But to spend little or no time with God is really telling Him (and ourselves) that He doesn't matter, and that everyone and everything else is more important to us than He is! Yet He is the ONLY one who gives us our value. We gain our confidence, self-worth and direction from our Lord who knit us together in our mothers' wombs (see Psalm 139:13). The God of the universe used His hands to make us perfectly in His image, and He wants us to rest in His perfect love. "Friends" or online popularity will NEVER satisfy us—only His love will satisfy. But, if you don't spend time making Him your "friend"—your very BEST friend—you can't experience that selfless, perfect love.

I know death is stalking me, and I know that I don't have the time to do everything I want to do, so I try to make the most of the limited time I have. When we allow the Lord God to direct our lives, He miraculously ensures that our time is well spent. But we must always have our "spiritual ears" tuned in.

 Teri: I am a Christian, but after reading this note I realize that I compartmentalize my life too much. I go to youth group on Wednesday night and church on Sunday morning. Once in a while, I participate in youth events and trips, or I pick up my Bible, but I turn on my computer and check my Facebook for a minimum of an hour every day. Obviously it would be easier for me to be influenced by my friends online, because I am spending more time with their thoughts and opinions than I am with God's truth. I need to reassess.

Comment On This · Love This · Share with Friends

Jon: Thanks for pointing out that social networking time isn't bad—we just have to find a healthy amount of time so we keep perspective.

Comment On This · Love This · Share with Friends

Pam: Absolutely! I enjoy social networking too! But, like everyone else, I must keep my time and value grounded in God so that He is most important, and I can view myself through the truth of His Word!

Comment On This · Love This · Share with Friends

Pam: The amount of time you spend and everything you post on social networking sites have a direct effect on yourself and others. Make sure you use this technology wisely!

Comment On This · Love This · Share with Friends

Chapter 8

Running the Race to Win: How to Fuel Up for the Marathon

 Pam: We have spent a lot of time looking at the dangers of the media and online social networking. Now let's take some time to encourage one another, sharing how we've been able to use media, technology and the talents we have been given to impact our world in positive ways.

Comment On This • Love This • Share with Friends

 Emily: I love using Facebook as a way to witness for Jesus! It's a great way to share verses and Christian song lyrics, write status updates about what God is doing in my life, and re-post news stories that have to do with my faith. I have especially loved using the recent news stories about abortion and Planned Parenthood to let people know the truth about the value of EVERY LIFE. I hope that my friends on Facebook will be drawn to Jesus when they see my status updates, because that's all that really matters—telling people about how amazing He is!

Comment On This • Love This • Share with Friends

 Trista: I use Facebook, Twitter and my YouTube channel to witness to others. I'm constantly putting up Bible verses and inspirational quotes. That's started some good conversations, and I praise the Lord for that. I have many non-Christian friends who I know see my Bible verses. Sometimes it's kind of intimidating, because maybe they won't like me as much if I'm a "Bible girl," but I know that it brings Him glory, and that means it's worth it!

Comment On This • Love This • Share with Friends

 Katie: I use Facebook all the time to share Bible verses, build up and encourage others in Christ, and spread the truth about Jesus and His Word. I know media can be used positively and negatively, and I love being able to use it in different ways to glorify God!

Comment On This • Love This • Share with Friends

Theresa: I want to make a difference, but sometimes I feel like I'm not "prepared" enough to be so public about my faith—or worse yet, what if someone thinks I'm crazy?

Comment On This · Love This · Share with Friends

Pam: God has uniquely gifted each of us. He gives us passion and purpose that are perfectly tailored to our personalities, our talents and our journeys. Without a doubt, there will be many times in our lives when we will wonder, *What is He doing? How will He ever use this particular experience in my life for His purpose?* But somehow, when we finally get the opportunity to look back, things begin to make sense, and we can see His hand in every "U-turn" and "detour."

It's important to remember that EVERYONE can make a difference, regardless of age. First Timothy 4:12 very clearly states, "Don't let anyone look down on you because you are young, BUT SET AN EXAMPLE for the believers in speech, in conduct, in love, in faith and in purity" (emphasis added). You can do this in your everyday life, and today's social networking resources provide opportunities to do it in new, exciting and far-reaching ways.

I want to challenge you to use EVERY available resource to do good for others and to share God's love with a lost world. God wants EVERYTHING YOU DO to glorify HIM. In 1 Corinthians 10:31, Paul says, "So whether you eat or drink or whatever you do, do it all for the glory of God."

Are you an artist? Glorify God through your art! Are you an actor? Praise Him and reflect His glory in your craft! Are you a musician? Sing and play His praises, making a JOYFUL noise to Him! Are you a dancer? Dance with joy for the King of kings!

If glorifying God with your life sounds strange, or you don't do it out of fear of being called a "wacko," maybe you need to ask some deep questions about your relationship with your Creator! If you truly know Him, you will WANT to shout of His love from the mountaintops.

The God of the universe knew you before He even formed you. He sanctified you, or set you apart, and has a specific plan for you (using your God-given gifts) to be "a prophet to the nations" (Jeremiah 1:4-5). That same God longs for a relationship with you RIGHT NOW. He loves you more than you could ever imagine! John 3:16 says He loves you so much He sent His only Son, Jesus, to DIE for YOUR sins so that you could spend eternity with Him in heaven! Even though we all have sinned and fall short of glorifying Him with our lives (see Romans 3:23), God has made a way for our sins to be forgiven and for us to be reconciled to Him through Jesus! That is why Jesus died!

Have you personally received God's gift of salvation in a life-transforming way, or have you just said the words to make your parents or pastor or someone else happy? If you have never truly received God's gift of salvation—if you have never accepted Christ's death on the cross for your sins and received forgiveness—then STOP right here! Today, right now, you can receive God's free gift of salvation!

"Everyone who calls on the name of the Lord will be saved" (Romans 10:13). EVERYONE includes you. "Will be saved" doesn't mean maybe, or might—it means WILL be saved. In Luke 18:13, the sinner prayed: "God, give mercy. Forgive me, a sinner" (*THE MESSAGE*). Now is your opportunity to pray:

> *Oh God, I know I am a sinner. I believe Jesus was my substitute when He died on the cross. I believe His shed blood, death, burial and resurrection were for me. I now receive Him as my Savior. I thank You for the forgiveness of my sins, the gift of salvation and everlasting life through Your merciful grace. Amen.*

You might be thinking, *Surely, it cannot be that simple.* Yes, it is that simple! It is scriptural. It's God's plan. Believe in Jesus and receive Him as Savior today. If you just prayed this for the first time, we'd love to hear from you! Please write to me through my website (www.pamstenzel.com) or contact me on Facebook! I would love to encourage you and welcome you to the family!

Comment On This · Love This · Share with Friends

 Lindsey: Hey, Theresa! I saw your post to Pam and wanted to encourage you as a fellow teenage sister in Christ to stand strong for God and speak out in His name. As a girl, I have found one of the best social networking places of encouragement to be *Susie Magazine*. Susie Shellenberger is the editor of this totally awesome magazine that is always filled with WONDERFUL articles pertinent to us. It's really helped deepen my faith, and once you subscribe, you become part of an online global sisterhood that connects you with other girls of faith and helps you live out the Christian life. Check it out at www.susiemag.com.

Comment On This · Love This · Share with Friends

Theresa: Thanks! I will!

Comment On This · Love This · Share with Friends

Kristin: When I was at mass, my priest told us that the Pope is encouraging them to use social media to get the word out. I thought it was super cool that the Church sees media as an evangelism opportunity. It reinforced that these media tools are not anti-God, but rather gifts from God to be used in unique, powerful ways.

Comment On This · Love This · Share with Friends

Pam: Awesome! Churches and ministries of all kinds are really creating a presence online, and it is helping to bring more visibility to God's truth. I know that I have "liked" the fan pages of many congregations, crisis pregnancy centers and other ministries on Facebook, and I LOVE seeing their posts. SO MANY hearts can be changed through media ministry!

Comment On This · Love This · Share with Friends

Pam: "We are what we repeatedly do. Excellence, then, is not an act, but a habit" (Aristotle).

Comment On This · Love This · Share with Friends

Dane: I love YouTube, and I've become really inspired by this boy named Chase Ravenscraft. He posts about all different topics and has Scriptures that go with them. It's really awesome. Not only is it a creative way to share about Christ, but he is also a TEEN changing the world! You can find his stuff at www.youtube.com/myjourneyisHIS.

Comment On This · Love This · Share with Friends

Pam: Thanks for sharing the link! What a great way to use video evangelism to "go and make disciples of all nations" (Matthew 28:19)!

Comment On This · Love This · Share with Friends

Jocelyn: I repeatedly post song lyrics and videos on my Facebook page. Recently I posted "Everything Falls" by Free. My cousin is a Jehovah's Witness, and about five minutes after I posted it, he commented on the video, saying he couldn't believe he just watched the whole video, but he was confused that it was a Christian song talking about love. I replied that it was a love song—a song about God's love. LOL. He wasn't very excited about my answer, but I was very glad that I got to tell him about God's love through that song. Facebook allowed that opportunity to share a message that I know he wouldn't have been open to any other way!

Comment On This · Love This · Share with Friends

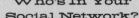
 Pam: GREAT story. One of the best aspects of media is that it is non-threatening. Anyone can listen or watch in private, without feeling like they are being pressured. By posting these Christian songs, you are showing why you have such intense love for God and how deeply He loves those who see your posts. Well done!

Comment On This · Love This · Share with Friends

Hannah's Story

 I have a goal to make a difference in every country in the world, and I am blogging about it! So far I have reached about 11 countries. On my blog you can see my progress, learn about my goals and passions, and learn about ways that you can make a difference too! Every time I make a post, it goes directly to Twitter and Facebook.

I am also an advocate for Compassion International. I sponsor two kids through Compassion and correspond with five more. I post about Compassion a lot on my blog, and I also promote the organization in my hometown and surrounding area.

Reaching people internationally is a huge passion of mine. I think my generation does not believe that they can make a difference, but with all the networking tools available to us, WE CAN! I want to tell my peers about these great ways to glorify God and challenge them to make a difference for Him!

 Joni: We kick off the season of Lent each year by making a crown of thorns. Using a salt dough recipe,[1] my family puts "thorns" in the crown and then pulls them out whenever one of us does something thoughtful or kind for someone else. The hope is that all of the thorns will be out by Easter, at which point we decorate the crown with jewels for our risen King. I always post pictures of this family activity on Facebook so that others can see them and think about Jesus' sacrificial love for us. I pray it helps the people who see it to go and live out His love for others to see!

Comment On This · Love This · Share with Friends

 Pam: What a great family tradition!

Comment On This · Love This · Share with Friends

📰 **Newsflash:** More than 30 billion pieces of content (links, stories, posts, photo albums and other items) are shared each month on Facebook.[2] Is what you are adding to that total drawing people closer to God?

Tenley: I'm an artist and a Christian. While most of my work has a modern feel (it's not overtly Christian), it is pure and cool and a great way to show the gifts He's given me to the masses. When I get done with new paintings, I always post them on Facebook for people to check out.

Comment On This · Love This · Share with Friends

Pam: The Bible tells us to be unashamed for Christ (see Romans 1:16), and so I think it is awesome that by sharing your gift you are encouraging others to do the same. Continue to be grateful for and proud of the talent He gave you!

Comment On This · Love This · Share with Friends

Note: Follow Your Dream. My friend Colin Hearn (who is the president of Enlighten Communications and therefore also my "boss") is a professional actor and involved in theater today. I love his words of encouragement for you!

Ever since I was a young boy, I wanted to go into the performing arts; it was my dream! Over the last 25 years, I have been very fortunate to have been able to live out my dream in many different ways.

It has not always been smooth sailing, but I wanted to stick with my goal to be a performer and to do it to the best of my ability. I did not and still do not want to settle for second best. I love these words from the heart of an artist: "When we do things that are excellent the world sits up and notices. Then we can point them to God who created us and gifted us and loves us" (anonymous).

There is nothing wrong with aiming high in what we do. In my craft, this is something I always want to do for myself, as well as for the theater companies I have had the opportunity to direct and the productions I participate in.

Christian artists can sometimes get a bad rap that what we produce is second best, which is why we must constantly strive to prove the critics wrong and be excellent in all we do.

I love encouraging young actors and performers to go and live out their dreams—and I always remind them not to leave their faith at the door. We need to be true to what we believe and stand strong in our faith and values. Get all the teaching you can, learn from those around you, and become the best you can be, so people will look up and take notice. Then we can point them to the One who created us!

Colin Hearn's Bio: Colin was born in Lambeth, London, in the United Kingdom. He trained at the Guildhall School of Music and Drama and has been a part of numerous productions throughout the United Kingdom and the United States. His most recent theater works include *A Christmas Carol*, the musical (Mr. Fezziwig); *1776*, the musical

(Benjamin Franklin); *West End to Broadway* Review *Show*; *Little Mary Sunshine* (Billy Jester); *The Wizard Of Oz* (The Wizard); *Carousel* (Mr. Snow); *The Marriage of Figaro* and Verdi's *Aida*. He also is part of the musical theater and improvisation company, Theater Off the Cuff (www.theateroffthecuff.com), with whom he has performed all over the USA, UK, Australia and Africa.

Sheila: I tweet a verse of Scripture every day. It is a simple act, but to do it repeatedly has held me accountable to reading God's Word, and it has also brought that Word to my followers on Twitter. Being faithful in this has helped me walk the walk and not just talk the talk.

Comment On This · Love This · Share with Friends

Pam: What a wonderful ritual! You are a light. Keep shining brightly for Him!

Comment On This · Love This · Share with Friends

Kraig: My friends and I make Fluffy Lemon Tree videos that we upload to YouTube. They are just silly, without a huge point, but they are clean and make our friends laugh. We've also used our skills to help with some projects that are actually important (such as promoting books like this one!). It is fun to see a hobby make people smile. I hope I get the opportunity to do more!

Comment On This · Love This · Share with Friends

Pam: Very cool! Glorifying Christ doesn't have to mean directly saying His name. Rather, glorifying Christ comes through doing what is right and pure. Secular projects, when they are clean, fill the mind with POSITIVE things—and who can't use a laugh?! Good for you!

Comment On This · Love This · Share with Friends

📝 **Note: The Parable of the Buried Talents (Matthew 25:14-28).** Please take a minute to read this passage. Jesus is teaching in parables, as He often does, to illustrate a spiritual lesson. Here He tells the story of a master who leaves his servants in charge as he travels for an extended period. He gives to each servant according to his ability. Five bags of gold to one, two to another and one to the last. (The original Greek word for what the *New International Version* of the Bible describes as a "bag of gold" is literally translated as "talent." One "talent" in Jesus' time would be the equivalent of 20 years' worth of a day laborer's wage, so five talents was an awful lot of money!) The servant with five bags doubled what the master had entrusted to him, as did the servant with two, but the last servant, out of fear, buried his one bag. When the master returned, that servant was only able to bring him the one bag he had been given in the first place.

The master praised the first two servants, but scolded the third servant, who seemed to "blame" the master himself for his fear of losing the money entrusted to him. Jesus wanted His followers to realize that they had each been given "talents" from their Father in heaven, and that God expects us to take that which we have been given and USE it for HIS KINGDOM, so that on the day we see Him face to face, we will be able to bring to Him the fruits of our labor.

We have opportunities, every day, to multiply what Christ has entrusted to us. Matthew seems to make a special point of noting that the master gave to each servant according to his ability. He already knew which servants would be most industrious, but he expected all to show some industry. The "amount" that you start with is not nearly as important as the "growth" on His "investment" that you bring to the Lord at the end of your life!

What "talents" have you received from God? Music? Art? Communication? Writing? Teaching? Acting? Intellect? Now I ask, how are you using your "talents" and gifts for the Kingdom? Are you multiplying your gifts, or have you buried them in the ground, afraid to lose or misspend what the Master has entrusted to you?

Todd: Thanks for bringing clarity to that passage. I think often we are so afraid of others making fun of us that we put our peers' thoughts first. This really helps me remember that I answer to God, not to them, and I need to live my life accordingly.

Comment On This · Love This · Share with Friends

Lola: God gave me the gift of writing poetry. Even though I don't always know what people will think of it, I often write about my life experience—and how God sees me through it—and then I post what I've written as a note on Facebook. I pray that as I use this gift, others are encouraged.

Comment On This · Love This · Share with Friends

Pam: In a world filled with junk, media has given us lots to celebrate!

Comment On This · Love This · Share with Friends

Emma: I love how after school I can head to the gym, turn on my iPod filled with Christian songs, and refocus. When I walk out, I feel refreshed and ready to be the face of Jesus in a broken world.

Comment On This · Love This · Share with Friends

Colton: I check the newest stuff on GodTube each day. How awesome that as a culture, we've come from purely secular media sites to one meant solely for video evangelism! My fave is the stand-up comedian Tim Hawkins. Oh my gosh, the guy's delivery is impeccable. I literally laugh out loud while I'm watching his stuff. Faith-focused and worth a laugh count as a double bonus in my world!

Comment On This · Love This · Share with Friends

 Jayson: I just got back from the movie *Soul Surfer.* If you haven't seen it, go to it—you will love it! It is the story of a girl who rebuilds her life after a shark attacks her on her surfboard. The cool thing is that it isn't "Hollywoodized" in the sense of focusing on the gruesome attack. Rather, it is about the rebuilding of her life and faith. It's honest. She questions God, but you see how even through tough stuff God is loving and good. Now that it is out on DVD I'm going to buy it, because it will be a good reminder during my own tough times.

Comment On This · Love This · Share with Friends

 Pam: YES! I love how this film brought an amazing message of hope in the face of adversity and testified to the power of faith in the midst of even life's most difficult moments. We are NEVER alone. God has plans for us to give us "hope and a future" (Jeremiah 29:11)! When we SHARE our stories, others can see His work in their lives too. I'm so thankful for this film's success!

Comment On This · Love This · Share with Friends

 Cooper: I tried to go with my family, but it was all sold out. The people at the theater said to get in, you need to buy tickets way in advance. I'm glad people are proving to Hollywood that we WANT the family-friendly movies.

Comment On This · Love This · Share with Friends

📰 **Newsflash:** Some accused *Soul Surfer* of being "too Christian" and doubted that audiences would respond. They were wrong. CinemaScore users gave the movie an A+, and the film took in $11.1 million in its opening weekend.[3]

 CJ: I watched your video in my college girls' class at church, and you have inspired me! I have always wanted to become a lawyer, focusing on prosecution and eventually becoming a judge. Since we started watching your videos, abortion has been on my heart a lot. I have now decided that I still want to get my law degree, but instead of prosecution, I want to focus on protecting the rights of those precious unborn babies. Abortion is nothing less than a premeditated murder and should be prosecuted the same way!

Comment On This · Love This · Share with Friends

Pam: Wow! We NEED lawyers who will fight for the right to LIFE for the unborn. I am so thankful to hear that after watching my talk and hearing my story, you will be a part of POSITIVE change. GOOD FOR YOU!

Comment On This · Love This · Share with Friends

 Regan: I am a football player, and I think *Facing the Giants* was a great movie. My team really isn't all that good, and sometimes I wonder why I bother playing. Other students harass us for our record, hardly anyone shows up to the games, and I hate to be a part of a "losing" anything. Who wants to stay on a sinking ship, right? But I really feel like God wants me to play football. Whenever I think about quitting, I get the worst feeling inside. I am decent at it, and I know that athletes can shine the light of Christ. I mean, look at Tim Tebow. That movie really helped me to see that I needed to let go of the outside noise and just focus on doing my best in each game and giving God glory afterwards. With God, all things are possible, and since I've changed my attitude, I can see Him blessing my decision. I'm part of a good group of guys—not just a bunch of partying jocks. The Bible says perseverance is necessary to build character, so I know He is working that in me too. We even won a game last week. Maybe our record is about to change???

Comment On This · Love This · Share with Friends

 Pam: KEEP listening to God, and He will carry out His perfect plan in your life. I'm so thankful that this film could be such an encouragement to you!

Comment On This · Love This · Share with Friends

Anna's Story

 I remember listening to "Set the World On Fire" by Britt Nicole around one of the lowest points in my life. Just after graduating from high school, I had decided to be part of Youth With A Mission (YWAM) for a year. During that time, I was stretched immensely in my faith. I was able to see the world through different eyes as I experienced many life-changing moments interacting with people I encountered in the States and overseas.

Shortly after, my mother had major surgery. She experienced many complications and had to stay in the hospital for over a month. Her body became really tired and weak. It was God's time to call her home.

Following her death, I was considering going to Hawaii to take a course in biblical counseling, but I was preoccupied. My father was praying about serving at a Nigerian Bible college for two years as a teacher. Honestly, I struggled with giving my father my blessing to leave me so soon after losing my mom. But I knew it was God's plan for my father to leave, because doors were opening right and left. I distinctly remember saying to my dad that it would be very hard with him being gone, but that I knew God would take care of me.

Hearing Britt Nicole sing that we are small but God is big, that we are weak but He is strong, and that He can take our dreams and give them wings gave me the courage to go to Hawaii for three months for schooling, and then to serve and teach in China for three months. Through Nicole's words, I gained confidence that there wasn't anything I couldn't do, and I was reminded how important it is to share Christ with people in the farthest lands.

Even though I believed those things, this was a very hard, stretching time for me as I served others. I was still grieving my mother's death, and I wasn't able to communicate with my dad in Nigeria much. Because I was on my own in so many ways, I really learned to rely on Christ as a "parent" during that time in my life. When I returned home to the U.S., I prayed for a way that I could reach out to my generation. The answer was to serve with a youth group. My prayer and dream, as Nicole's song says, was this: "I wanna set the world on fire until it's burning bright for You. It's everything that I desire, can I be the one You use?"

I had been home for about a month, recovering from my trip to China, when I received an early morning phone call from Nigeria. The person on the phone asked me if I was my father's next of kin and then proceeded to tell me that he had been killed in a public transportation accident.

Now, in this very dark place, I had a choice to make. Was this "Christian" thing really for me? Was I going to walk away from what I knew to be true? Over those next few weeks and months, many people prayed for me as I battled. But I knew I couldn't go forward without Christ in my life. With His help, I was able to continue doing the things I love instead of walking away from my faith.

Then, my earlier prayer about serving a youth group was answered. I was given the opportunity to serve as a youth intern for the summer. I was able to be real with the students, and they were able to hear who Christ is—in both good and bad times.

I'm now 25 years old, and I'm continually amazed to see how Christ can use me and teach me many things about His character! He is alive and real! I'm so thankful for the faith and action Britt Nicole's song has inspired in my life. Regardless of your age or circumstance, trust this assurance: "Lord, with You there's nothing I cannot do—nothing I cannot do!"

 Aimee: My experience with the benefits of Facebook has been very positive. I am able to network and communicate with people from all over the WORLD through Facebook. It has grown the ministry God has entrusted to me by leaps and bounds. I can simultaneously communicate with my people in Africa, India, Mexico, Germany and throughout the U.S. with ease! Without these valuable tools, very little of the international expansion of my ministry would have been possible. People are able to communicate with large groups of other people very quickly now, and as a result, communities are rising up to overthrow wicked leaders. If Facebook is sucking away people's time, that does not indicate that there is a problem with the technology itself; it just means it's a new aspect of life that needs to be more carefully monitored. People almost always end up wasting time in life, if not on Facebook then on TV or video games or taking naps. I personally think Facebook is a "better" waste of time than those other things if you can't think of anything productive to do at that moment.

Comment On This · Love This · Share with Friends

Jennifer: I don't have my own formal ministry. I'm only in high school. But Facebook has allowed me to keep up with lots of pro-life and abstinence ministries that I otherwise wouldn't. This helps me bring new information back to clubs at school and youth group so I can encourage others.

Comment On This · Love This · Share with Friends

Pam: Online social networking has definitely given us the ability to expand our spheres of influence. Everyone has a ministry that God has given them, and when they "broadcast" it through social networks, people everywhere can be inspired!

Comment On This · Love This · Share with Friends

Scott: I love music! Recently Josh Wilson used his musical talent to write and record a song that illustrates Matthew 25 beautifully. The song is called "I Refuse," and Wilson wrote it in response to the Nashville Flood of 2010. In the video, Wilson introduces the song by sharing the story of how the flood affected him, and how God convicted him to act in compassion rather than stand on the sidelines while others suffered. He sings about how sometimes it seems easier to stand by and watch—or, worse yet, move on like nothing is happening—but he doesn't want to be that person. He won't sit around and wait anymore. He will do something TODAY. This message always encourages me to be a person who gets involved.

Comment On This · Love This · Share with Friends

Pam: That song is an awesome testimony to being obedient to God's call.

Comment On This · Love This · Share with Friends

Scott: I think it is easy to forget that we are supposed to be the hands and feet of Jesus in our world. The words of this song remind us that we can't mask ourselves from the suffering of the world. Enough sitting back and hoping someone else will do the work. I started volunteering in a local soup kitchen because helping the poor is something I always hear about in church—and even though I'd like to think poverty doesn't exist, sadly, it does, big time. I finally realized that it was about time I acted on what I say I believe. What I found out is that although the lives of the people I went to help look completely different from mine, they still have a lot to offer in helping to teach ME about life.

Comment On This · Love This · Share with Friends

✒ **Note: Prayer of Commitment.** As you've read through this book, you've seen how media can sink you into a life of despair and harm your walk with God, or, if used positively, strengthen your faith and help you—and all those you touch—to live your faith out loud. It really is like food. It is a necessity and an ever-present part of life, but how much and what we consume make all the difference in terms of what comes out of our lives. I challenge you to read Proverbs 4:23-27 (printed below) and "personalize" it. Make it a prayer of commitment to being Christlike in your life and entertainment choices:

Proverbs 4:23-27
Above all else, guard your (MY) heart,
    for everything you (I) do flows from it.
Keep your (MY) mouth free of perversity;
    keep corrupt talk far from your (MY) lips.
Let your (MY) eyes look straight ahead;
    fix your (MY) gaze directly before you (ME).
(LET ME) give careful thought to the paths for your (MY) feet
    and be steadfast in all your (MY) ways.
Do not (LET ME) turn to the right or the left;
    keep your (MY) foot from evil.

Will you stand strong in doing what is right today? Will what you watch and listen to behind closed doors reflect character and integrity? Will you use social media to draw people closer to God? Will you use your talents to glorify Him? This is your chance!

Just this week, as I was finishing writing this book, my sister shared with me news of a tragedy that occurred in my hometown in Michigan. A wonderful man—a youth pastor, husband and father—and his infant son were taken from their family in a horrible house fire. When tragic events like this occur, I cannot help but ask God, "Why? Why did this husband, father and pastor, who was reaching this generation and using his life for Your glory, have to die?" It is another reminder that we are not promised tomorrow. I am reminded again today that EVERY day is precious! I am called to glorify God today. Tomorrow might not come.

I truly believe that God is raising up a generation like never before, with tools that no generation before them has ever possessed, to reach out and change our world. You are part of this amazing generation, and you can be part of God's work in the world right now. You don't have to finish Bible college or receive a fancy degree; YOU SIMPLY NEED TO GLORIFY GOD TODAY, right where you are, with the gifts and talents you have NOW! He has promised never to leave you or forsake you (see Hebrews 13:5). He will be right by your side! Take God at His word today! Don't wait to be pushed over the side of the boat while Jesus walks on the water towards you! Don't wait for God to send a giant whale to swallow you up and then vomit you out where He told you to go in the first place! Just say, "YES, Lord, I will go and do whatever you ask . . . TODAY."

Pam: Now GET OUT THERE AND CHANGE YOUR WORLD!!!!

Comment On This · Love This · Share with Friends

Endnotes

Chapter 1: Assess Your Media Health: Is a Diet Necessary?

1. "Sex and Tech: Results from a Survey of Teens and Young Adults" (Washington, DC: The National Campaign to Prevent Teen and Unplanned Pregnancy, 2008). http://www.thenationalcampaign.org/sextech/PDF/SexTech_Summary.pdf (accessed July 2011).
2. Victoria J. Rideout, M.A., Ulla G. Foehr, Ph.D. and Donald F. Roberts, Ph.D., "Generation M^2: Media in the Lives of 8- to 18-Year-Olds," The Henry J. Kaiser Family Foundation, 2010. http://www.kff.org/entmedia/upload/8010.pdf (accessed July 2011).
3. Ibid.
4. "AAP Media Mailing for June 14, 2010 Pediatrics," American Academy of Pediatrics News Room, June 14, 2010. http://www.aap.org/pressroom/aappr-june1410mailing.htm (accessed July 2011).
5. "Pearls in the Media Muck," Charisma, March 1, 2011. http://www.charismamag.com/index.php/component/content/article/1555-columns/30270-pearls-in-the-media-muck (accessed July 2011).

Chapter 2: Hollywood Serves Up Junk

1. Dick Rolfe, "That's Not Just Entertainment!" Charisma, February 22, 2011. http://charismanow.com/index.php/entertainment/30266-thats-not-just-entertainment (accessed July 2011).
2. The Dove Foundation, National Consumer Opinion Poll. http://www.dove.org/opinionpoll.asp (accessed July 2011).
3. Joe S. McIlhaney, Jr., M.D., and Freda McKissic Bush, M.D., *Hooked: New Science on How Casual Sex Is Affecting Our Children* (Chicago, IL: Northfield Publishing, 2008), pp. 39-40.
4. "Sexual Development and Health: Condoms," 4parents.gov, 2005. http://www.4parents.gov/topics/contraception.htm (accessed July 2011).
5. Kimberly Powers, *Escaping the Vampire: Desperate for the Immortal Hero* (Colorado Springs, CO: David C. Cook, 2009).

Chapter 3: *Jersey Shore, Teen Mom* Serving a Steady Diet of Big Macs

1. Rebecca A. Maynard, ed., *Kids Having Kids: A Robin Hood Foundation Special Report on the Costs of Adolescent Childbearing* (New York: The Robin Hood Foundation, 1996). http://www.robinhood.org/media/7490/khk.pdf (accessed July 2011).
2. *Preventing Unplanned and Teen Pregnancy: Why It Matters* (Washington, DC: The National Campaign to Prevent Teen and Unplanned Pregnancy, 2005). http://www.thenationalcampaign.org/why-it-matters/pdf/WIM_Full%20Set.pdf (accessed July 2011).
3. Michael J. Brien and Robert J. Willis, "Costs and Consequences for the Fathers," cited in Saul D. Hoffman and Rebecca A. Maynard, eds., *Kids Having Kids: Economic Costs and Social Consequences of Teen Pregnancy* (Washington, DC: The Urban Institute Press, 1997), pp. 95-143.
4. "'Teen Mom' Stars' Big Salaries Revealed," Huffpost Entertainment, October 28, 2010. http://www.huffingtonpost.com/2010/10/28/teen-mom-stars-big-salari_n_775543.html (accessed July 2011).
5. *Preventing Unplanned and Teen Pregnancy: Why it Matters.* http://www.thenationalcampaign.org/why-it-matters/pdf/WIM_Full%20Set.pdf (accessed July 2011).
6. Ray Fowler, "Statistics on Living Together Before Marriage," RayFowler.Org, April 18, 2008. http://www.rayfowler.org/2008/04/18/statistics-on-living-together-before-marriage/ (accessed July 2011).
7. Cassie Boorn, "Teen Mom," August 18, 2010. http://cassieboorn.com/2010/08/teen-mom/ (accessed July 2011).
8. "TV Reviews: *Jersey Shore*," Focus on the Family, *Plugged In Online*. http://www.pluggedin.com/tv/jkl/jerseyshore.aspx (accessed July 2011).

9. "Youth Risk Behavior Surveillance—United States, 2009," *Morbidity and Mortality Weekly Report*, vol. 59, no. SS-5 (Atlanta, GA: Centers for Disease Control and Prevention, 2010). http://www.cdc.gov/mmwr/pdf/ss/ss5905.pdf (accessed July 2011).

10. "Condom Warnings—Beware!!!" Pro-Life America. http://www.prolife.com/CONDOMS.html (accessed July 2011).

11. "11 Facts About Teens and STIs," DoSomething.org. http://www.dosomething.org/tipsandtools/11-facts-about-teens-and-stds.

12. "Our Say: Efforts to Reduce Teen Drinking, Drug Use Remain Essential," *The Capital,* April 8, 2011. http://www.hometownannapolis.com/news/opn/2011/04/08-03/Our-Say-Efforts-to-reduce-teen-drinking-drug-use-remain-essential.html (accessed July 2011).

13. "Statistics," Students Against Driving Drunk, January 2011. http://www.sadd.org/stats.htm (accessed July 2011).

14. Jeff Greenfield, "The Real Deal on Reality TV," CBS News, September 5, 2010. http://www.cbsnews.com/stories/2010/02/07/sunday/main6183037.shtml (accessed July 2011).

15. Ibid.

16. Andrew Malekoff, "Invizible kidz on the edge of 5 boroughz (poetry)," *Journal of Progressive Human Services*, 13:2, pp. 69-74.

17. Vicki Courtney, "Why I'm Quitting the Glee Club," October 26, 2010. http://vickicourtney.com/2010/10/why-im-quitting-the-glee-club/ (accessed July 2011).

18. Hollie McKay, "Prime Time TV 'Objectifies and Fetishizes' Underage Girls, Study Says," Fox News.com, December 16, 2010. http://www.foxnews.com/entertainment/2010/12/16/new-study-shows-images-sexualized-teen-girls-dominating-airwaves/# (accessed July 2011).

Chapter 4: My iPod Is Going Straight to My Thighs

1. "Ohio School Shooter Had Mental Problems," CBS News. http://www.cbsnews.com/stories/2007/10/11/national/main3356426.shtml (accessed July 2011).

2. Craig A. Anderson and Nicholas L. Carnagey, "Exposure to Violent Media: The Effects of Songs with Violent Lyrics on Aggressive Thoughts and Feelings," *Journal of Personality and Social Psychology,* vol. 84, no. 5, May 2003, pp. 960-971.

3. "GaGa: My songs are like sex," *The Sun*, March 10, 2009. http://www.thesun.co.uk/sol/homepage/showbiz/bizarre/usa/2310400/Lady-GaGa-talks-about-naughty-sex.html (accessed July 2011).

4. "Dirty Song Lyrics Can Prompt Early Teen Sex," MSNBC.com, August 7, 2006. http://www.msnbc.msn.com/id/14227775/ns/health-sexual_health/ (accessed July 2011).

5. Pam Stenzel and Melissa Nesdahl, *Nobody Told Me* (Ventura, CA: Regal, 2010).

6. Dr. C. M. Roland, editor of *Rubber Chemistry and Technology*, letter to the editor, *The Washington Times*, April 22, 1992, p. G-2.

7. "Condom Warnings—Beware!!!" Pro-Life America. http://www.prolife.com/CONDOMS.html (accessed July 2011).

8. William C. Symonds, David Kiley, Tom Lowry and Kirstin Dorsch, "The Fashion of the Christ," Bloomberg Businessweek, May 23, 2005. http://www.businessweek.com/magazine/content/05_21/b3934018_mz001.htm (accessed July 2011).

Chapter 5: I've Been Gaming So Long I Have a Mountain Dew High

1. Suzanne Choney, "Most Younger Net Users Get There Wirelessly," MSNBC.com, February 3, 2010. http://www.msnbc.msn.com/id/35206710/ns/technology_and_science-tech_and_gadgets/ (accessed July 2011).

2. Iowa State University, "Risks, Consequences of Video Game Addiction Identified in New Study," *ScienceDaily*, January 19, 2011. http://www.sciencedaily.com/releases/2011/01/110119120550.htm (accessed July 2011).

3. Ed Bradley, quoted in Rebecca Leung, "Can a Video Game Lead to Murder?" *60 Minutes.* http://www.cbsnews.com/stories/2005/06/17/60minutes/main702599.shtml (accessed July 2011).

4. Ben Berkowitz, "Most Teens Play Violent Video Games, Study Says," *Washington Post*, September 16, 2003. http://www.lionlamb.org/news_articles/Washington_Post_Grand_Theft.htm (accessed July 2011).

5. Mark Boal, "The Kill Team: How U.S. Soldiers in Afghanistan Murdered Innocent Civilians," *Rolling Stone*, April 14, 2011, pp. 56-69.

6. "Study: Violent Video Game Play Makes More Aggressive Kids," *U.S. News*, March 3, 2010. http://www.usnews.com/science/articles/2010/03/03/study-proves-conclusively-that-violent-video-game-play-makes-more-aggressive-kids (accessed July 2011).

7. Lt. Col. Dave Grossman and Gloria DeGaetano, *Stop Teaching Our Kids to Kill* (New York: Crown Publishers, 1999).

8. "National Commission to STOP the NEW VIOLENCE: Address by Col. David Grossman," The Schiller Institute, May 20, 2000. http://www.schillerinstitute.org/new_viol/ctte_grossman.html (accessed July 2011).

9. Steven Johnson and Victoria Schlesinger, "This Is Your Brain on Video Games," *Discover*, July 9, 2007. http://discovermagazine.com/2007/brain/video-games/article_view?b_start:int=2&-C (accessed July 2011).

10. Scott Firestone's website is www.youthministry.com.

Chapter 6: Pornography Addiction Is Worse Than Chocolate

1. "Teens: Imitating 87 Hours of Watching Porn," Clean Cut Media, April 20, 2009. http://www.cleancutmedia.com/articles/teens-imitating-87-hours-of-watching-porn (accessed July 2011).

2. Mike Celizic, "Her Teen Committed Suicide Over 'Sexting,'" *TODAY*, MSNBC.com, March 6, 2009. http://today.msnbc.msn.com/id/29546030/ns/today-parenting/ (accessed July 2011).

3. Emily Friedman, " 'Sexting' Teens May Face Child Porn Charges," ABC News, February 12, 2009. http://abcnews.go.com/US/story?id=6864809 (accessed July 2011).

4. Jan Hoffman, "A Girl's Nude Photo, and Altered Lives," NDTV, March 27, 2011. http://www.ndtv.com/article/world/a-girl-s-nude-photo-and-altered-lives-94443 (accessed July 2011).

5. Deborah Feyerick and Sheila Steffen, " 'Sexting' Lands Teen on Sex Offender List," CNN, April 7, 2009. http://articles.cnn.com/2009-04-07/justice/sexting.busts_1_phillip-alpert-offender-list-offender-registry?_s=PM:CRIME (accessed July 2011).

6. "Portage Teen Arrested For 'Sexting' As Two Girls Apparently Sent Him Naked Pictures," *HuffPost Chicago*, April 14, 2011. http://www.huffingtonpost.com/2011/04/14/portage-teen-arrested-sexting_n_849058.html (accessed July 2011).

7. "Sex and Tech: Results from a Survey of Teens and Young Adults" (Washington, DC: The National Campaign to Prevent Teen and Unplanned Pregnancy, 2008). http://www.thenationalcampaign.org/sextech/PDF/SexTech_Summary.pdf (accessed July 2011).

8. Anastasia M. Northrop, "Pope John Paul II's Theology of the Body" (Cheyenne, WY: Resurrection Publications, 2003). http://www.jp2.info/Theology_of_the_Body.pdf (accessed July 2011).

9. Jim Graves, "The My House Initiative," *The Catholic World Report*, January 2011. http://www.catholicworldreport.com/Item/356/the_my_house_initiative.aspx (accessed July 2011).

10. David Knowles, "Addiction and Pornography," Natural Health Web. http://www.naturalhealthweb.com/articles/Knowles1.html (accessed July 2011).

11. Bobby Maddex, "The Naked Truth: An Interview with Dr. Judith Reisman," *Salvo*, Spring 2007. http://www.salvomag.com/new/articles/salvo2/2maddex.php (accessed July 2011).

12. William J. Bennett, *The Book of Virtues* (New York: Simon and Schuster, 1993), p. 48.

13. Richard Restak, M.D., cited in Bill Moyers, "Mind and Body: The Brain," PBSTV, February 1993.

14. "Pornography Statistics," Family Safe Media, 2005 and 2006 data. http://www.familysafemedia.com/pornography_statistics.html (accessed July 2011).

15. Ibid.

16. Stephen Arterburn and Fred Stoeker, with Mike Yorkey, *Every Young Man's Battle* (Colorado Springs, CO: WaterBrook Press, 2002).

17. Shannon Ethridge and Stephen Arterburn, *Every Young Woman's Battle* (Colorado Springs, CO: WaterBrook Press, 2004).

Chapter 7: I Think I Look Like a Model—Facebook Is Feeding My Ego!

1. Amanda Lenhart, Kristen Purcell, Aaron Smith and Kathryn Zickuhr, "Social Media and Young Adults," Pew Internet and American Life Project, February 3, 2010. http://www.pewinternet.org/Reports/2010/Social-Media-and-Young-Adults.aspx (accessed July 2011).

2. Jan Kern, "Internet Addiction? Millions of Americans Admit to Compulsive Internet Use," November 17, 2008. http://jankern.com/2008/11/17/internet-addiction/ (accessed July 2011).

3. "Is Social Networking Changing Childhood," Common Sense Media, August 10, 2009. http://www.commonsensemedia.org/about-us/news/press-releases/social-networking-changing-childhood (accessed July 2011).

4. "Facebook for Parents," Common Sense Media, November 19, 2010. http://www.commonsensemedia.org/facebook-parents (accessed July 2011).

5. Hamid Sirhan, "1,200 Tweets per Second (and Other Interesting Twitter Stats)," FutureLab, March 16, 2010. http://www.futurelab.net/blogs/marketing-strategy-innovation/2011/03/1200_tweets_second_and_other_i.html (accessed July 2011).

6. "Frequently Asked Questions: How Many Videos Are on YouTube?" YouTube. http://www.youtube.com/t/faq (accessed July 2011).

7. "Sex and Tech: Results from a Survey of Teens and Young Adults" (Washington, DC: The National Campaign to Prevent Teen and Unplanned Pregnancy, 2008). http://www.thenationalcampaign.org/sextech/PDF/SexTech_Summary.pdf (accessed July 2011).

8. Michael Seamark, "Paedophile Postman Used Facebook and Bebo to Groom up to 1,000 Children for Sex," *Mail Online*, 28 May 2010, http://www.dailymail.co.uk/news/article-1282157/Facebook-grooming-How-pervert-postman-used-site-groom-hundreds-children.html (accessed July 2011).

9. Theresa Gutierrez, "Boy Apparent Target of Child Predators on YouTube," WLS-TV/DT, April 19, 2011. http://abclocal.go.com/wls/story?section=news/local&id=8082605 (accessed July 2011).

10. Christine Lagorio, "You're 15: Who's Watching You Online?" *CBS News*, February 26, 2010. http://www.cbsnews.com/stories/2006/06/08/gentech/main1696408.shtml (accessed July 2011).

11. Rochester Institute of Technology (2008), "Statistics," Internet Safety Awards. http://www.internetsafetyawards.org/pdfs/internet.statistics.2010.pdf (accessed July 2011).

12. Ibid.

13. Lindsey Tanner, "Docs Warn About Teens and 'Facebook Depression,'" MSNBC, March 29, 2011. http://www.msnbc.msn.com/id/42298789/ns/health-mental_health/ (accessed July 2011).

Chapter 8: Running the Race to Win: How to Fuel Up for the Marathon

1. "Salt Dough Recipe," Catholics United for the Faith. http://www.cuf.org/familyresources/saltdoughrecipe.asp (accessed July 2011).

2. "Statistics," Facebook. http://www.facebook.com/press/info.php?statistics (accessed July 2011).

3. "'Soul Surfer' Big Hit at Box Office," *Charisma*, April 12, 2011. http://www.charismamag.com/index.php/news/30672-soul-surfer-big-hit-at-box-office (accessed July 2011).

Resources

Chapter 2: Hollywood Serves Up Junk
Walk the Talk Youth Ministries
Kimberly Powers
http://wttym.org/Walk_the_Talk_Youth_Ministries/Home.html

Chapter 3: *Jersey Shore, Teen Mom* Serving a Steady Diet of Big Macs
Vicki Courtney
http://vickicourtney.com/
www.virtuousreality.com

Chapter 5: I've Been Gaming So Long I Have a Mountain Dew High
Killology Research Group
Col. David Grossman
http://www.killology.com/index.htm

YouthMinistry.com
Scott Firestone IV
http://www.youthministry.com/

Chapter 6: Pornography Addiction Is Worse Than Chocolate
Dr. Judith Reisman
http://drjudithreisman.com/

Chapter 7: I Think I Look Like a Model—Facebook Is Feeding My Ego!
Jan Kern
http://jankern.com/

Janie Lacy
http://janielacy.com/

Chapter 8: Running the Race to Win: How to Fuel Up for the Marathon
Theater Off the Cuff
Colin Hearn
www.theateroffthecuff.com

About the Authors

Pam Stenzel for years was on the "front lines" as director of Alpha Women's Center, a counseling center for women undergoing crisis pregnancies. Her experiences taught her that before teen pregnancy and STD rates could decline, attitudes of teens toward sex first had to change. Desiring to bring about that change, Pam started speaking nationally full-time. Today, she is in great demand both in the United States and in other countries such as Mexico, Canada, Australia, Ireland and South Africa. Drawing from her personal story, as well as her visits with teens around the world, Pam talks about the consequences— both physical and emotional—of sex outside of marriage. It's been her experience that to-day's young people, if given the facts, are fully capable of making good, healthy decisions.

To book Pam for your conference or your community, go to **www.pamstenzel.com** and click on "**Bring Pam**." To order DVDs and curriculum for both church and public schools, go to **shoppamstenzel.com**. If you have a question or story you want to share with Pam, go to **www.pamstenzel.com** and click on "**Ask Pam**."

Follow Pam on twitter.com/Pam_stenzel
Facebook Page: "Fans of Pam Stenzel, speaker and author"

Melissa Nesdahl, after seeing the effects of pre-marital sex on her peers, began educating area teens at a crisis pregnancy center about the physical, emotional and spiritual risks of sex outside of marriage and the benefits she experienced firsthand in choosing absti-nence until marriage. Melissa recognized that when students understood who they were in Christ, they chose the best for their body and future. Combining her passion to write with her love of sharing truth, Melissa routinely updates her website, writes product and cur-riculum with Pam Stenzel, is a monthly contributor for MODsquad (Mothers of Daughters), and shares other writing projects and articles.

To visit Melissa's website, go to http://melissanesdahl.blogspot.com/
To follow Melissa on Twitter, go to http://twitter.com/#!/MelissaNesdahl

Join the *Who's in Your Social Network?* fan page on Facebook and give us your feedback! We would love to hear from you!!!

ENLIGHTEN

perspective ◆ education ◆ abstinence

www.enlightencom.com

Enlighten Communications, Inc. is a not-for-profit organization whose goal is to provide structured abstinence education that empowers adolescents to create a new healthy perspective of at-risk behavior.

Enlighten Communications provides resources, healthy programs and perspectives regarding teen pregnancy and sexually transmitted diseases while promoting a clear message of abstinence until marriage.

Enlighten Communications, along with Pam Stenzel, have initiated programs and activities that continue to change the way our society views character issues pertaining to at-risk behavior. The United States and countries abroad have embraced our healthy perspective program initiatives that include the sale and distribution of educational resources, Internet resources, speaking engagements for youth, seminars for parents and educators and accredited medical seminars.

Enlighten Communications' main objectives in the following areas have been accomplished since 2001:

- Delay sexual onset
- Decrease the number of teen pregnancies
- Abate additional sexually risky behavior
- Increase the number of adolescents who remain sexually abstinent until marriage

Let's face it: Today's teenagers are in a whole new arena when it comes to sexually transmitted diseases. They're facing consequences that teens from previous generations couldn't even imagine. That is why it is so important to make sure that today's teens hear straight talk . . . about sex, about the consequences, and about the life-and-death choices that they meet every single day.

Pam connects and is a powerful voice on the side of responsibility and morality in a culture war that offers kids all too many voices on the other side. She delivers a shocking message to kids—you are not out of control sex maniacs. Waiting has some nice rewards, and avoids some terrible price tags.

Sean Hannity, Radio and TV Host
FOX News, WABC Radio

Sex Has a Price Tag, by Pam Stenzel and Crystal Kirgiss, focuses on abstinence, sexual urges, biblical definitions, physical consequences and diseases, taboo subjects and where teens can go for help. Young readers will be freed of confusion and embarrassment and will be equipped to meet the challenges of this all-important topic that looms in every teen's life. Trade paper book, 160 pages (Youth Specialties Student-Ware Book, published by Zondervan).

Today, people are faced with a raging plague of sex related problems. Pregnancy, sexually transmitted diseases and rape statistics are at all-time highs. Even so, today's society encourages sexual activity, and young people must have a compelling reason to commit to sexual abstinence. In the *Sex Still Has a Price Tag* DVD, world-renowned abstinence educator Pam Stenzel combines her personal story and extensive pregnancy counseling experience in a hard-hitting look at the consequences of sexual activity outside of a monogamous, lifetime relationship. Running time approx. 1 hour 10 minutes. Also available with Spanish subtitles.

Today's teens have not been told the whole truth about the consequences of their choices when it comes to sex! The culture hands them a daily dose of sex through music, television, movies, the Internet, social sites and texts while never showing the devastation that sex outside of marriage leaves behind. This is a four-part DVD series that also comes with a leader's guide on CD-ROM with reproducible handouts for students. This series is a fantastic teaching tool for churches, youth groups, teen Bible studies and Christian schools! Running time approx. 3 hours.

In a culture that increasingly throws its hands up, tells parents that they can't make a difference in the lives of their kids, and even belittles their influence with "Patsy" commercials . . . Pam Stenzel wants parents to know that THEY DO MATTER! She stresses that they are their kids' PARENTS, not their friends, and the values they pass on to their children and the faith they act out will make a difference in the lives of their children not just here on earth but also for all eternity. This DVD contains a question and answer section. Running time approx. 1.5 hours.

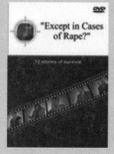

Have you ever heard someone say, "I am against abortion, except in cases of rape"? Maybe you have said or thought this very thing yourself. This brand-new DVD powerfully addresses that question by introducing you to the very people who have been faced with that decision or who are survivors. You will hear the testimonies of women who have been raped and those who were conceived in rape. This DVD will forever change your heart and mind and is a powerful tool for your church, pregnancy center, or pro-life organization. Running time approx. 1 hour.

If you like *Sex has a Price Tag/Time to Wait for Sex,* you will love *Sex Ed—No Screwing Around.* This is a unique product that showcases testimonies of students and a newly married couple as well as Pam Stenzel and other counseling professionals who deal with the struggles teens face in relationships. This DVD is an engaging, magazine-style production that is great to use in your classroom or other venue to generate discussion about the importance of abstinence until marriage. Available in faith-based and public school formats and includes a teacher's guide. Running time approx. 30 minutes.

Available at shopPamStenzel.com

Also Available from
Pam Stenzel

Nobody Told Me
Pam Stenzel and Melissa Nesdahl
ISBN 978.08307.56537
ISBN 08307.56531

When Pam Stenzel started counseling in pregnancy centers more than 20 years ago, she heard one thing time and time again: "I didn't know. If somebody would have told me this would happen to me, I would have made a different choice." After nine years of listening and learning from young women and men facing unplanned pregnancies, positive STD results and heartache from broken relationships, Pam knew that someone needed to start telling the truth about the consequences when sex isn't right. *Nobody Told Me* gives you the information you need to make smart choices about sex, relationships and your future. You'll find answers to questions submitted by young people just like you, plus guidelines to guarantee your physical, emotional and spiritual health. Get the facts about sex and learn how to do it right.

Available at Bookstores Everywhere!
Go to **www.regalbooks.com** to learn more about your favorite
Regal books and authors. Visit us online today!

Regal
God's Word for Your World™
www.regalbooks.com